Pupil's Book 1

ICT InteraCT
for KS3

The Dynamic Learning student website contains activities which are cross-referenced throughout the book. To access the website follow the instructions printed on the inside front cover.

Pupil's Book **1**

ICT InteraCT
for KS3
Bob Reeves
Consultant: Alan Plumpton

HODDER
EDUCATION
AN HACHETTE UK COMPANY

The Publishers would like to thank the following for permission to reproduce copyright material:

Photo credits: p.13 and **21** Photodisc; **p.15, 40, 51, 66, 67, 82, 83, 84** and **104** Steve Connolly; **p.17** © David Newham/Alamy; **p.45** Alan Thornton/Stone/Getty Images; **p.61** ©Don Mason/Corbis; **p.71** ©Patrick Giardino/Corbis; **p.85** Volkswagen UK; **p.96** *t* Data Harvest Group Ltd.; **p.97** iRobot Corp./AP/PA Photos; **p.107** © Lucas Schifres/Corbis.

Acknowledgements: p.5 *l* BBC Music Magazine, *r* © NME/IPC+Syndication; **p.26, 28** and **29** Google; **p.96** *bl* Economatics Education, *br* © Keep I.T. Easy http://www.flowol.com; **p.106** *l* www.chatdanger.com, ChildNet International, *r* www.thinkuknow.co.uk, Child Exploitation and Online Protection Centre.

t = top, *b* = bottom, *l* = left, *r* = right

Every effort has been made to trace all copyright holders, but if any have been inadvertently overlooked the Publishers will be pleased to make the necessary arrangements at the first opportunity.

Although every effort has been made to ensure that website addresses are correct at time of going to press, Hodder Education cannot be held responsible for the content of any website mentioned in this book. It is sometimes possible to find a relocated web page by typing in the address of the home page for a website in the URL window of your browser.

Hachette UK's policy is to use papers that are natural, renewable and recyclable products and made from wood grown in well-managed forests and other controlled sources. The logging and manufacturing processes are expected to conform to the environmental regulations of the country of origin.

Orders: please contact Hachette UK Distribution, Hely Hutchinson Centre, Milton Road, Didcot, Oxfordshire, OX11 7HH. Telephone: +44 (0)1235 827827. Email education@hachette.co.uk. Lines are open from 9 a.m. to 5 p.m., Monday to Friday. You can also order through our website: www.hoddereducation.co.uk.

© Bob Reeves 2008
First published in 2008 by
Hodder Education,
an Hachette UK Company
Carmelite House, 50 Victoria Embankment
London EC4Y 0DZ

Impression number	20
Year	2025 2024 2023 2022

Cover photo Corbis
Illustrations by Richard Duszczak, Tony Jones/Art Construction.
Case Study introduction artworks by Magic Software Pvt. Ltd.
Typeset in 13.5/15pt ITC Officina Sans by Stephen Rowling/Springworks
Produced by DZS Grafik, Printed in Bosnia & Herzegovina

A catalogue record for this title is available from the British Library

ISBN: 978 0340 940 976

CONTENTS

INTRODUCTION

Welcome to ICT InteraCT Book 1. The book has six main *modules*:

> Module 1 Presenting information
> Module 2 Selecting, refining and using information
> Module 3 Modelling
> Module 4 Data handling
> Module 5 Control
> Module 6 ICT in the real world

Each of these modules has several *units*. The book is designed so that every unit takes up either two or four pages of the book. There are 32 units in total, which sounds a lot, but the course is designed to be flexible and your teacher will tell you what they'd like you to cover!

The ICT InteraCT Dynamic Learning student website contains an electronic copy of the book and lots of other resources that you'll need to boost your knowledge and understanding of ICT, and to develop your practical skills. Your teacher will show you the electronic version of the book and you will find that its layout looks exactly the same as the printed pages. The electronic version works a bit like a web page because it has lots of links in it that will open up other resources.

You will notice that all the pages have various icons on them. On the electronic version of the book, these icons will link you to the other resources. Before you get started, it is worth having a quick look at how the pages are laid out and what each of the icons mean.

Here is a list of the icons you will come across in this book:

 Written Tasks

 Practical Tasks

 Skills Tutorials

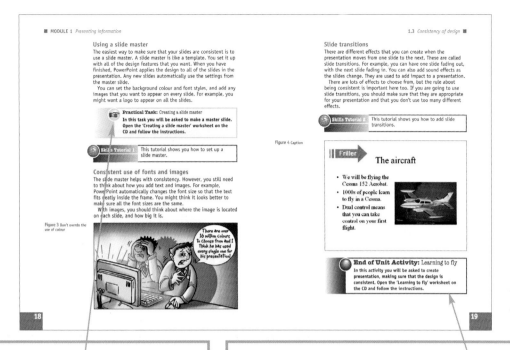

Practical Tasks: These are small tasks where you will be asked to do something on the computer.

End of Unit Activities: These are larger tasks where you can show how well you have understood what you have learnt during the unit.

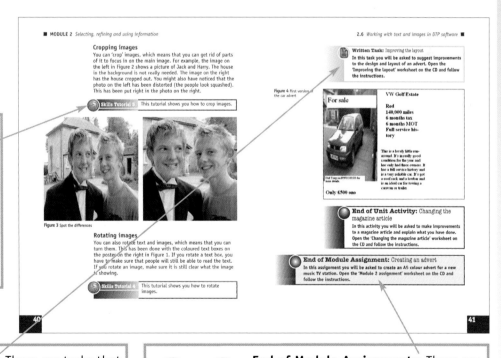

Skills Tutorials: These are 'how to' guides that will show you how to do things on the computer.

Written Tasks: These are tasks that you don't need a computer for. Your teacher might ask you to do these for homework, or you might do them if you have a lesson when you are not in the computer room.

End of Module Assignments: These are mini-projects that might take a lesson or more to complete. There is one at the end of every module. You can show how well you have understood what you have learnt in the module.

1 PRESENTING INFORMATION

Case Study introduction

Meet John Senior and John Junior. They are father and son. Like many dads and their sons, they agree on some things but not on others. They both like to watch the news but they argue over which channel to watch. John Senior likes News 24 and the Sunday morning news programmes and John Junior likes Newsround.

> **Q** What are the main differences in the way that a news story is presented on each channel?

They sometimes listen to the radio together in the car on the way to school. John Senior likes Mature FM. John Junior prefers to listen to Youth FM.

> **Q** What are the main differences in the way information is presented on each radio station?

They both like music but, as you might have guessed by now, they don't like the same music. John Senior has a copy of the *BBC Music Magazine*, which is the world's best selling classical music magazine. John Junior is a bit more up-to-date than his dad. He likes rock music, so he reads the *NME*.

Figure 2 *BBC Music Magazine*

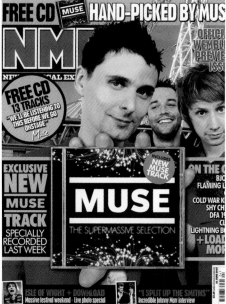

Figure 3 *NME* magazine

Q What differences do you notice about the style of the two magazines?

Figure 4 John Junior in his ICT lesson

John Junior is in his ICT lesson. He's good at ICT. Mrs Wendell, the ICT teacher, has asked him to create a slideshow using PowerPoint. It's Open Evening soon and parents will be visiting each department to see what they do. Mrs Wendell thought a PowerPoint slideshow would be a good idea. John Junior opens up PowerPoint and starts designing the slideshow. After a few minutes he's got his first two slides.

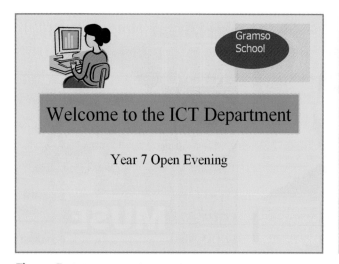

Figure 5 Slide 1 – pupil version

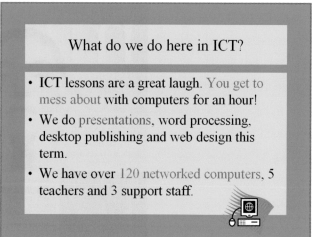

Figure 6 Slide 2 – pupil version

> **Q** Do you think that John Junior's presentation is appropriate for what it is going to be used for?

John Junior starts to think about the argument he had the night before with his dad. He realises that the people who will be watching this presentation will be just like his dad. This makes him think again about his presentation. His dad won't like the way that some of the information is presented. Other adults might not like it either.

> **Q** What changes could be made to John Junior's presentation to make it more appropriate for an adult audience?

John Junior goes back to the keyboard and starts to make some changes. After a few minutes the slides now look like this.

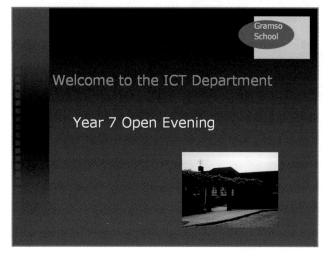

Figure 7 Slide 1 – parent version

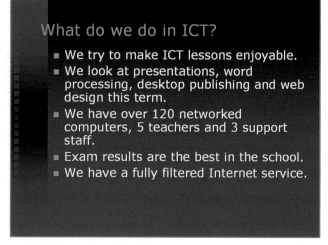

Figure 8 Slide 2 – parent version

Q What changes has John Junior made to the presentation?

Figure 9 Open Evening

What do we do in ICT?

- We try to make ICT lessons enjoyable.
- We look at presentations, word processing, desktop publishing and web design this term.
- We have over 120 networked computers, 5 teachers and 3 support staff.
- Exam results are the best in the school.
- We have a fully filtered Internet service.

On Open Evening, the parents sit and watch the presentation. John Junior feels a bit nervous because they are all watching the presentation that he made. He did all the things that he thought his dad would like, but now he's worried that it seems a bit boring. At the end of the presentation, all of the adults clap. John Junior asks his dad what he thought of the presentation. His dad tells him that he thought it was exactly right for the occasion and that he is proud of his son for doing such a good job.

Figure 10 Father and son after the presentation

1.1 Evaluating a presentation

In this unit you will learn how to:
> **Decide what you like and don't like about a presentation**
> **Consider purpose and audience**
> **Identify what makes a good presentation**

Introduction to presentations

There are lots of different ways of presenting information to people and you may have talked about some of these already. In this unit, we look at PowerPoint presentations. These are sometimes called slideshows. Slideshows combine text, images and sounds onto separate pages, called slides. Slideshows can have any number of slides in them.

People make slideshows for all kinds of reasons. They are really useful if they are projected onto a big screen while a person is doing a talk. Another option is for people to sit and watch them on their own computer.

All presentations have a *purpose* (a reason for showing it) and an *audience* (the people who will be viewing it). Have a look at the 'LaughAid 1 presentation'. This is being shown in schools and gives ideas about how pupils can raise money for charity. Two of the slides are shown below.

Figure 1 Two slides from the 'LaughAid 1' presentation

Written Task: LaughAid review

In this task you will be asked to review a presentation. Open the 'LaughAid review' worksheet on the website and follow the instructions.

Purpose

Every presentation is made for a reason:

> to entertain, e.g. a slideshow about your hobbies to be shown to your friends
> to inform, e.g. a slideshow shown to parents about GCSE options
> to persuade, e.g. a slideshow used by a charity to encourage people to raise money.

In Unit 1.2, you will make your own presentation. When your presentation is finished you should check that it is suitable for its purpose.

Audience

Think about the programmes that you have seen on TV recently or the websites you have visited. Did you notice how they were made in a certain style? For example, what about the news? The way that it is presented on BBC News 24 is very different from the way it is presented on Radio 1 or on a programme like Newsround. You might never have seen News 24. If not, why is that? The reason is because it is made in a style that will appeal to the audience.

When you make a presentation, you must be very clear about who the audience is. When your presentation is finished you should check that it is suitable for this audience.

Features of a good presentation

When you make a presentation, you need to make sure that you don't make the mistakes that LaughAid did. Here are a few things you should check:

> Is the purpose clear?
> Have you got the main message across?
> Is it suitable for the intended audience?
> Have you got the right amount of text on each slide?
> Is the use of language suitable?
> Have you used colour appropriately?
> Have you used suitable images and sounds?

Look at the 'LaughAid 2 presentation'. You can compare it to the original version to see how it has improved. It will also help you with the End of Unit Activity.

 End of Unit Activity: Choosing ICT for GCSE

In this activity, you will be asked to think about the audience and purpose for a presentation and suggest ways of improving the presentation. Open the 'Choosing ICT for GCSE' worksheet on the website and follow the instructions.

1.2 Creating a basic presentation

In this unit you will learn how to:
> **Work with templates**
> **Add text and images to slides**
> **Run a slideshow**

Presentation basics

In this unit, we look at how to create a simple presentation. As you saw in Unit 1.1, a presentation is made up of slides, which the audience views one slide at a time. The slides can contain text, wordart, images, video, animations or sound. Slideshows are sometimes designed to be shown while a person is talking and sometimes they are used on their own.

In this unit, you are going to create a presentation all about yourself. You can then show this to your classmates. As you create your slideshow, it is very important to keep in mind the purpose and the audience; in this case:

> **Purpose:** to tell your classmates about yourself
> **Audience:** your classmates.

You should read through this unit before starting your presentation.

Working with templates

PowerPoint has a selection of slide 'templates', or layouts, that you can use. Figure 1 shows the layouts:

Figure 1 PowerPoint slide layouts

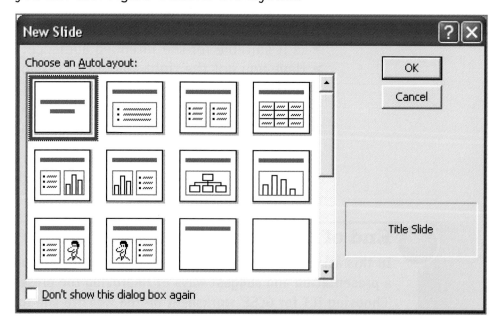

You need to choose the layout that is most suitable for the information you are presenting. This presentation will have at least four slides:

> Slide 1: Title
> Slide 2: Personal details: age, height, hair colour, which town or village you live in, etc.
> Slide 3: Hobbies
> Slide 4: Family and friends.

You can add other slides later if you wish.

| Skills Tutorial 1 | This tutorial shows you how to create new slides in PowerPoint. |

Written Task: Designing a presentation

In this task you will be asked to create a rough design for a presentation. Open the 'Designing a presentation' worksheet on the website and follow the instructions.

Adding text

Now that you have your design, you can start to make your slideshow. You need to think carefully about how much text to put on each slide and what font sizes, styles and colours you use. We saw how bad slideshows can look in some of the examples in Unit 1.1. You can follow these simple guidelines:

> Do not put too much text on a slide.
> Use a font size that is big enough, probably size 20 and above.
> Do not use too many different types of font.
> Do not use too many colours of font.
> Make sure the colour of the font stands out from the background colour.

| Skills Tutorial 2 | This tutorial shows you how to add text to a slide. |

Figure 2 Make sure that your presentation is easily readable

Adding images

The great thing about slideshows is that they can be 'multimedia'. This means that, as well as text, you can add images, animations, video and sound. We are now going to look at adding images.

You can get images from several places. The images might be pictures or photographs. You could get them from:

> clipart
> the Internet
> photographs you have taken on a digital camera
> photographs or images that you have scanned with a scanner.

You should choose the image that is most appropriate. For example, a photograph of yourself would be more appropriate in your presentation than a clipart image.

Figure 3 Clipart images

Skills Tutorial 3 This tutorial shows you how to add images to a slide.

Running the slideshow

When your slideshow is complete you should check it carefully as you would with any piece of work. This means proof-reading as well as spell-checking. When you run the slideshow, the slides will be shown one after another. You can set the slides to change automatically after a few seconds, or get the viewer to click the mouse themself to move on. When you move from one slide to the next this is known as a 'transition'.

You have to choose the right transition for your slides. This depends on the **purpose** and the **audience**. For example, as people read at different speeds, you might set your slideshow to change slides only when clicked by the user.

 **Skills Tutorial 4** This tutorial shows you how to run a slideshow and change transitions.

Figure 4 An example slide

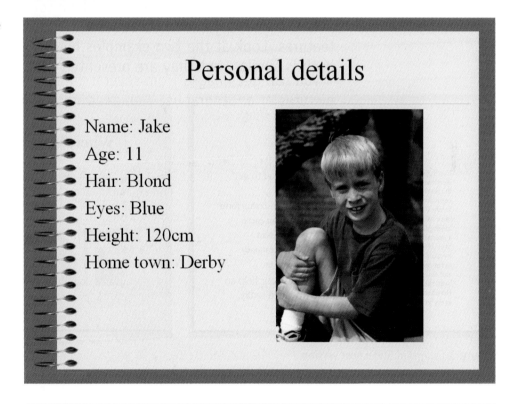

 End of Unit Activity: All about me

In this activity you will be asked to create a presentation all about yourself. Open the 'All about me' worksheet on the website and follow the instructions.

1.3 Consistency of design

In this unit you will learn how to:
> **Get a consistent design**
> **Use a slide master**
> **Use slide transitions**

Presentation design

In Unit 1.2, you learned how to create a basic presentation using slide layouts, text and images. In this unit we look at how we can improve the overall design of the presentation. This unit also shows you how to set up slide transitions, which is the way that the slideshow moves from one slide to the next.

It is very important to try to achieve *consistency* of design. This means that every slide in a slideshow shares the same design features. Look at the two examples below. The information in both is similar, but they are presented very differently:

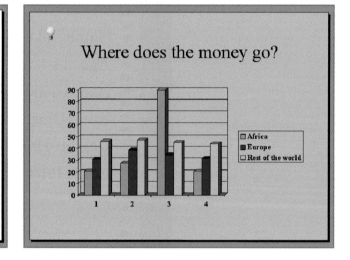

Figure 1 LaughAid Slideshow version 1

You can see that in Slideshow 2, the slides share some common design features:

> the background colour
> the font style and colour used for the heading
> the font style and colour used for the bullet points
> the use of the clipart in the top right-hand corner.

Figure 2 LaughAid Slideshow version 2

Written Task: Consistent design

In this task you will be asked to compare two presentations. Open the 'Consistent design' worksheet on the website and follow the instructions.

Figure 3 Slides from the Written Task about consistent design

Using a slide master

The easiest way to make sure that your slides are consistent is to use a slide master. A slide master is like a template. You set it up with all of the design features that you want. When you have finished, PowerPoint applies the design to all of the slides in the presentation. Any new slides automatically use the settings from the master slide.

You can set the background colour and font styles, and add any images that you want to appear on every slide. For example, you might want a logo to appear on all the slides.

 Practical Task: Creating a slide master
In this task you will be asked to make a master slide. Open the 'Creating a slide master' worksheet on the website and follow the instructions.

 **Skills Tutorial 1** | This tutorial shows you how to set up a slide master.

Consistent use of fonts and images

The slide master helps with consistency. However, you still need to think about how you add text and images. For example, PowerPoint automatically changes the font size so that the text fits neatly inside the frame. You might think it looks better to make sure all the font sizes are the same.

With images, you should think about where the image is located on each slide, and how big it is.

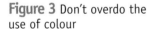 **Figure 3** Don't overdo the use of colour

Slide transitions

There are different effects that you can create when the presentation moves from one slide to the next. These are called slide transitions. For example, you can have one slide fading out, with the next slide fading in. You can also add sound effects as the slides change. They are used to add impact to a presentation.

There are lots of effects to choose from, but the rule about being consistent is important here too. If you are going to use slide transitions, you should make sure that they are appropriate for your presentation and that you don't use too many different effects.

 Skills Tutorial 2 | This tutorial shows you how to add slide transitions.

 **End of Unit Activity:** Learning to fly
In this activity you will be asked to create a presentation, making sure that the design is consistent. Open the 'Learning to fly' worksheet on the website and follow the instructions.

Figure 4 Slide from the 'Learning to fly' presentation

The aircraft

- We will be flying the Cessna 152 Aerobat.
- 1000s of people learn to fly in a Cessna.
- Dual control means that you can take control on your first flight.

AN38E5 Alamy Images

1.4 | Information, images and sound

In this unit you will learn how to:
> **Select appropriate information to put into a slideshow**
> **Select appropriate images to put into a slideshow**
> **Select appropriate sound to put into a slideshow**

Purpose and Audience

In Units 1.1, 1.2 and 1.3 we looked mainly at the *design* of slides. In this unit we start to think more about the *content* of slides. The content is the actual information that is presented in the slideshow. We will look at how to decide what information, images and sounds to use in a slideshow, depending on its purpose and audience.

You have probably seen some slideshows yourself and thought:

> Why are they telling me this?
> I don't understand that slide.
> There is too much information. I can't take it all in.

Figure 1 Make sure the content is correct for your purpose and audience

If this has happened to you, it is because whoever did the slideshow did not think carefully enough about the purpose and audience.

When you create a slideshow, the two questions you should ask yourself are:

> What is this for? (Purpose)
> Who is this for? (Audience)

Selecting information

You need to decide what you want to tell people and how much information to give them. You also need to decide how you want to tell them. This will depend on the purpose and the audience. For example, let's say you were asked to do a presentation to your friends called 'What I did last summer'. Now imagine you had to present it to your parents and teachers. Would you change any of the information?

Sometimes you have a lot of information to tell people about in your presentation. If this is the case, you might have to edit the information, or summarise it so that there is not too much.

 Written Task: Editing information
In this task you will be asked to edit some information to make it suitable for a presentation. Open the 'Editing information' worksheet on the website and follow the instructions.

Selecting images

Carefully chosen images may help your audience understand what you are telling them much better than words can. They can also bring a presentation to life. Look at the two slides on the next page, which describe what a computer tower and keyboard are. Which one is easier to understand?

There are all sorts of images available. You can have cartoon-style graphics such as the ones in clipart libraries; you can have images that you have scanned; you can use photographs that you have taken yourself or found on the Internet. Many images belong to the people that created them. This is called *copyright*. You are not allowed to use someone else's images unless you have asked them first.

A computer tower and keyboard

A computer tower is the main part of a computer. It is the 'box' that you put on the floor or next to the computer. You connect it with leads to your keyboard and screen. It has a kind of 'tray' on the front that slides out so that you can put a CD or DVD in. It also have sockets where you can plug things in like a digital camera.

The keyboard has lots of keys on it. You type on the keys and the letters are displayed on the screen.

A computer tower and keyboard

Figure 2 A picture is worth a thousand words

When choosing images, you need to think about various things:

> What type of image should I use?
> Is the image relevant to what I am presenting?
> Does the image show exactly what I want it to?
> Does it need cropping or re-sizing?
> Have I used too many images?
> Am I allowed to use this image or does it belong to someone else?
> Should I say where I got the image from?

Badly chosen images can make a presentation look really bad, so choose carefully.

Selecting sounds

Sound is a great way of adding impact to your presentation. You should select sound in the same way as you do images. This means thinking about what sounds are relevant to the presentation and asking yourself the same questions as you ask about images. You can record sounds yourself, get them from a CD or DVD, or from the Internet. Some clipart libraries have some sounds too.

As with images, you need to know who actually owns the sound clip. For example, you are not allowed to create a copy of a chart CD and use that in your presentation without asking whoever owns the copyright.

 **Skills Tutorial 1** | This tutorial shows you how to add images and sounds to a presentation.

Figure 3 Images from the Summer Fun holidays folder on the website

 End of Unit Activity: Holiday presentation

In this activity you will be asked to create a presentation for a holiday. Open the 'Holiday presentation' worksheet on the website and follow the instructions.

1.5 | Refining a presentation for a different audience

In this unit you will learn how to:
> **Adapt an existing presentation for a different audience**

Introduction

In this unit, you look at an existing presentation and then change it so that it will appeal to a completely different audience. For example, the Summer Fun Holiday Company that we looked at in the last unit has different types of holidays: some for older people; some for families; some for young adults; and some for children.

A presentation for older people would be very different to one that they did for young adults. The information would be different and so would the design of the slideshow.

Thinking about the audience

A good exercise in thinking about different audiences is to compare a young audience (your age) to an old audience (your parents' age).

Older people tend to like presentations that:	Younger people tend to like presentations that:
> Do not use too many colours	> Are colourful
> Have a consistent layout	> Have lots of graphics and sounds
> Are well written, with no slang	> Are written in a less formal style
> Have clear, good-sized fonts	> Have a range of fancy fonts

This is not a full list and you may be able to think of other features that might appeal to people of your age that would not appeal to older people. For example, have you noticed how your teachers hate u using txt language :-(.

Written Task: Audiences

In this task you will be asked to create two presentations for different audiences. Open the 'Audiences' worksheet on the website and follow the instructions.

Figure 1 French slideshow for Year 7 pupils

Figure 2 French slideshow for adults

Adapting a presentation

Look at the slide shown in Figure 1. It is part of a slideshow about a school trip. A Year 7 pupil created it to show to her classmates.

You can see that the pupil has:

> used lots of bright colours
> used lots of different font styles and colours
> written it in a 'chatty' way using some slang words (and a spelling mistake)
> included some information that is not really relevant
> made an image out of shapes.

If the pupil was asked to adapt this slide to show to an adult audience, she might:

> use fewer colours
> add a more suitable image
> re-write it in a more formal style
> delete the irrelevant information.

The finished slide would look more like the one shown in Figure 2.

 End of Unit Activity: A day in the life

In this activity you will be asked to create a presentation for a school parents' evening, adapting it for different audiences. Open the 'A day in the life' worksheet on the website and follow the instructions.

End of Module Assignment: Creating a school presentation

In this assignment you will be asked to create a presentation for Year 6 pupils who will be starting the school next year. You will have to adapt the presentation to make it suitable for their parents. Open the 'Module 1 assignment' worksheet on the website and follow the instructions.

SELECTING, REFINING AND USING INFORMATION

························ ## Case Study introduction

This is Remy. He is the editor of the school magazine. Every month he decides what articles and news stories he is going to put into the magazine, which is bought by pupils. There are about 200 copies of the magazine printed every month. Remy has been in charge for about a year now and he has a good reputation for writing interesting and well-balanced articles. This month he has decided to write an article about whether playing computer games too much can be bad for you.

Figure 1 Remy reading the school magazine

> **Q** Where could Remy get his information from for this article?

Remy starts to plan the article. He decides that he will interview some people to find out what they think about it. He also needs some other sources of information. He would like some other opinions and some facts if he can find any. He decides that the Internet is a good place to start.

> **Q** How can Remy use the Internet to find what he wants?

Remy loads up a search engine and types in: 'Are computer games good or bad for you?'.

He decides to limit his search to UK websites and presses Search. After a few seconds the first page of results is shown. He checks for the number of results. There are over two million. He starts to read the descriptions of some of the sites. Lots of them don't seem that relevant.

> **Q** Why has Remy got over two million results? Why are some of the websites he has found not relevant? How could Remy improve the results?

Figure 2 AttackGames.org

http://www.AttackGames.org

Attack Games.org – the home of the best-selling game: "Nuke the planet", the ultimate battle for the earth.

Computer games are not bad for you.

There is a lot of talk about how computer games are bad for you. We are here to tell you that this is all nonsense. Here at "Attack Games" we have been making computer games for over 5 years. We have people testing our games for 8 hours a day, and they are all perfectly fine.
None of them is overweight and they all have good eyesight. We do not know what all the fuss is about.
Game on!

It takes Remy a while, but eventually he finds some relevant information among the results. He finds the site shown in Figure 2.

He reads it and it seems that it has some very clear evidence that computer games are not bad for you at all, even if you play them a lot.

> **Q** Can Remy trust this information? Why might it be unreliable?

Remy is now ready to turn the information into a magazine article.

> **Q** What software should Remy use? What should he do before he starts using the software?

Remy decides that he will plan his magazine article before he starts. He sits down with a pen and paper and sketches out a design. He knows that he has to get the right mix of text and images and that the layout is very important.

> **Q** How can Remy design and write the article so that it will appeal to Remy's readers?

Once Remy is happy with the design, he starts to use Publisher, which is a desktop publishing (DTP) package. You can find Remy's finished article on the website.

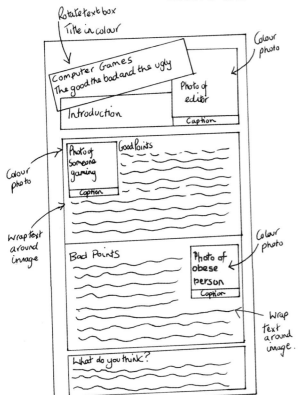

Figure 3 Sketch of the magazine article

2.1 Researching information

Introduction to searching the Internet

There are many sources of information. The Internet is one of them. It contains millions of web pages covering every topic you can think of. This gives us two main problems:

> There is so much information it is hard to find what you want.
> You cannot be sure that the information is reliable.

This unit and Unit 2.2 focus on how you can find the information you need. Unit 2.3 looks at how you can judge whether it is reliable and trustworthy or not.

Search engines

You probably have websites that you visit on a regular basis. If this is the case, you probably know the 'address', or you may have saved it in your 'Favourites' list. This is a very efficient way of getting to a website. The problem is that you usually don't know the address. In these cases you need a search engine, such as Google.

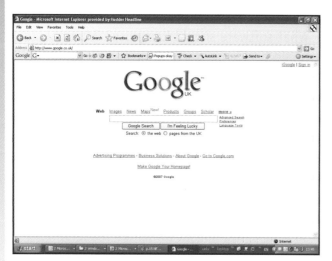

Figure 1 Google search engine

This is how a search engine works:

1 You type in 'keywords' that describe what you are looking for.
2 The search engine then searches the Internet.
3 A few seconds later, it shows you a list of all of the sites it has found that might be relevant.
4 The number of 'hits' is shown in the top right-hand corner. This is the number of websites it has found.
5 You click on the links to go to the site.

The problem is that you usually get thousands or even millions of hits. You can't possibly look through all of these websites to find the information you need. Ideally, your search produces only a small number of hits.

Skills Tutorial 1

This tutorial shows you how to use a search engine.

 Practical Task: Searching the Internet

In this task you will be asked to search the Internet. Open the 'Searching the Internet' worksheet on the website and follow the instructions.

Basic search techniques

Let's say you want to donate some money to charity. You open the search engine and type:

> 'Charity' – this would give you millions of hits.
> 'How do I donate money to charity?' – this would also give you millions of hits and is a slow way of doing it as you have to type in so many words.

You need to think carefully about the keywords that you use. You might need to use two or three words to describe what it is you are looking for. For example, if you know that you want to donate to the NSPCC, you should type 'NSPCC donations' into the search engine.

 Written Task: Searching for information

In this task you will be asked to think about different sources of information. Open the 'Searching for information' worksheet on the website and follow the instructions.

Looking through the results

Once you have your list of hits, you can click on the links to go to the websites. These may not contain the information you need. Just because a site is at the top of the list does not mean it is the most relevant. Read the short description of the site before you click on it. You also need to scan the website when you get to it to see if it is relevant. You can then close the site and go back to your search engine to refine your search.

 End of Unit Activity: Finding information

In this activity you will be asked to find information about teenagers' health. Open the 'Finding information' worksheet on the website and follow the instructions.

2.2 | Refining search techniques

Learning Objectives	**In this unit you will learn how to:** > **Refine a search to find relevant information**

Advanced search techniques

In the last unit, we looked at how you can type keywords into a search engine. If you choose the right keywords, you get a smaller number of 'hits' and the website you are looking for is likely to be at the top of the results. The example we used before was the NSPCC. They are a large charity and have their own website, so typing in NSPCC brought their site to the top of the list.

In other cases, the information might be more difficult to find. For example, what if we wanted to find out about the Loch Ness Monster? Can we find out whether it is real or fake? What websites can we use to find out?

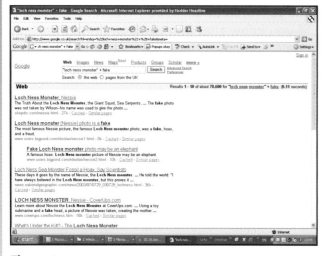

Figure 1 Refining a search

Refining text searches

You could type in 'Loch Ness Monster' or even just 'Nessie' and you will get lots of results. Most of these would be relevant. However, there will be thousands of hits. We are trying to find evidence to prove that she is real or not, so we could try:

"Loch Ness Monster" + fake

or

"Loch Ness Monster" + proof

The use of speech marks is important:

> If you type in Loch Ness Monster, it will find all websites with ANY of those three words, in any order. So it might list websites about any monsters.
> If you type "Loch Ness Monster" it will find websites with *all* of those words in *that* order. This will reduce the number of hits and make the search more relevant.

The use of the + sign means that the website must also contain the following word. The number of hits goes down to around 650, if you type:

"Loch Ness Monster" + fake

You can put as many words in as you like. For example:

"Loch Ness Monster" + fake + evidence

This will take the number of hits down to around 270. You can also use the − sign to exclude a word from the search. For example, the keywords we have typed in so far might include links to online bookshops trying to sell us books about the Loch Ness Monster. You could type:

"Loch Ness Monster" + fake + evidence -books

This would stop these sites being listed in the results.

Most search engines also have an 'advanced' search option that allows you to do the same kind of searches without having to use the speech marks and + signs.

Skills Tutorial 1

This tutorial shows you how to use the advanced search options in Google.

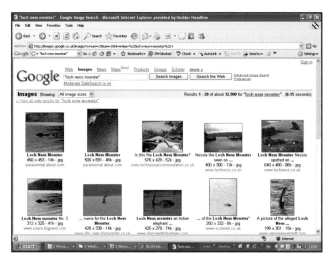

Figure 2 Searching for images

Searching for images

Most search engines, including Google, have an image search option. These work in the same way as a normal search. You type in keywords as usual, but you click 'Images' instead of 'Web'. The results page then contains lots of thumbnail images that match the keywords. You can click on the thumbnail to view the website where the image came from.

If you know that it is an image that you want, this is a more efficient way of finding it, rather than scanning through lots of different websites.

Written Task: Search techniques

In this task you will be asked to use different key words when using a search engine. Open the 'Search techniques' worksheet on the website and follow the instructions.

End of Unit Activity: Does Nessie exist?

In this activity you will be asked to search the Internet to find out whether the Loch Ness monster exists. Open the 'Does Nessie exist?' worksheet on the website and follow the instructions.

2.3 | Checking information

In this unit you will learn how to:
> **Check whether information is reliable, accurate or biased**

Introduction to checking information

In Units 2.1 and 2.2, we searched for information that was suitable for its purpose. Once we have found the information, we have to check that it is:

> Reliable – this means that we can trust the information
> Accurate – this means that it contains no factual errors
> Not biased – this means that it shows both sides of the story.

Read the following statements about child health.

Statistics confirm that children who watch more than two hours of television a day at the weekend risk becoming obese adults.

Source: Institute of Child Health and Great Ormond Street Hospital, 2006

This child health thing is a big fuss about nothing. Children are just as healthy now as they were when I was a girl.

Source: Mrs M Brown, Parent, 2006

We have reduced the salt content of crisps and they are now better for you.

Source: A crisp manufacturer, 1999

Which of these statements are you most likely to believe? Why?

Written Task: Reliable statements

In this task you will be asked to decide whether various statements are reliable or not. Open the 'Reliable statements' worksheet on the website and follow the instructions.

When you find some information, whether it is on the Internet or from another source, there are some questions you can ask yourself:

Who has supplied the information?

> If it is a well-known organisation you might be more likely to trust the information supplied.

> If the information is on a website that you have never heard of, then you need to find out more about it.

> You can check the web address. For example, '.gov' means that it is a government website. '.co.uk' or '.com' are most likely to be businesses, but they could belong to anyone.

What is their purpose in providing the information?

> Lots of websites exist just to persuade you to buy something. If this is the case, the information may be biased to make those products look better than they are.

> Other websites are there to inform, educate or entertain. Some sites that claim to inform and educate might only be giving one side of the story. For example, an anti-nuclear power website will probably not explain the benefits of nuclear power.

> There are lots of people who hold strong views about certain issues and these people use the Internet to get their message across. The information they put on their sites may be very biased.

Is the information up to date?

> Information can go out of date very quickly.

> Try to find the date that the information was created or when the website was last updated.

Can the facts be checked?

> It is risky taking all your information from one source, especially if you are not sure how reliable the source is.

> You should check the information with a source you do trust.

> You could also check several websites to see if you get the same information from each site.

End of Unit Activity: Evaluating information from websites

In this activity you will be asked to check whether information you find on websites is reliable, accurate or biased. Open the 'Evaluating information from websites' worksheet on the website and follow the instructions.

2.4 Designing a magazine article

Learning Objectives

In this unit you will learn how to:
> **Plan the design for a magazine article**
> **Select and refine the information you will use**

Introduction

In Units 2.1, 2.2 and 2.3, we looked at how to find information and how to check that it is reliable. We are now going to use that information to create a magazine article using desktop publishing (DTP) software. The article is for a magazine called *Elevenses*, which is aimed at people around your age.

You need to plan out:

> the design of the magazine article
> how much information is needed
> what information you are going to use.

You may not be able to include all of the information that you have found. You may need to change the way the information is written or summarise it so that it is suitable for the audience.

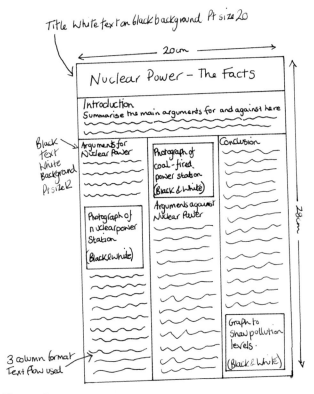

Figure 1 Sketch for magazine article

Design in DTP

We are going to use Microsoft Publisher to create the article. Publisher contains many pre-set layouts that you can use, or you can create your own. It uses 'frames', which can contain text or images.

This makes it easy to create a design, as you can decide on what frames you are going to have and what information they will have in them. The example in Figure 1 is a design for a magazine article about nuclear power. This appeared in a magazine aimed at older people. In Module 1, we looked at how you might design a presentation to appeal to a particular audience. You can apply what you learnt to DTP work as well.

Notice that the design is quite plain, with lots of text. It is also designed to be printed in black and white.

Written Task: Magazine layouts

In this task you will be asked to compare the layouts of two different magazine articles. Open the 'Magazine layouts' worksheet on the website and follow the instructions.

Selecting information

In Unit 2.1, you were asked to collect information that you needed for an article about whether teenagers are healthy. You now need to decide which of this information you are going to use. You should make sure that:

> you have the right amount of information for the space available

> the information is written in a style that is suitable for the audience

> the information you choose shows both sides of the argument.

You might have too much information, in which case you need to select the most appropriate, or summarise the information. You may not have enough information, in which case you will need to collect some more. You may also need to find some suitable images.

Figure 2 Call that a summary?

End of Unit Activity: Designing a magazine article

In this activity you will be asked to create a rough design for a magazine article and to get the information together for it. Open the 'Designing a magazine article' worksheet on the website and follow the instructions.

2.5 | Creating a magazine article using DTP software

Learning Objectives

In this unit you will learn how to:
> **Create a magazine article using DTP software**
> **Work with 'frames' to add text and images**
> **Use text flow**

Introduction

In this unit, you will create the magazine article that you designed in Unit 2.4. We will be using Microsoft Publisher, which can be used to create different kinds of publications, such as leaflets, posters, cards and even websites. This is the first of two units on using DTP software. This unit shows you the basics and Unit 2.6 looks at some of the additional features, such as layering, text-wrapping and working with images.

When you use word-processing software, such as Microsoft Word, you type straight onto the page. In Publisher, you have to put a frame on the page first and then put what you want into the frame. This makes it easier to create different kinds of publications as you can simply move the frames around to create your design.

You should remember that the purpose and the audience are important here, just as they were in Module 1 when you were creating presentations.

Skills Tutorial 1

This tutorial shows you how to get started in Microsoft Publisher.

Creating the layout

Publisher has five types of frame:

A Text: allows you to type in text.

▦ Table: allows you to enter a table.

✗ WordArt: allows you to create effects with letters.

🖼 Picture: allows you to add a picture from a file or paste one in.

🄰 ClipArt: allows you to add an image from the ClipArt gallery.

Written Task: Working with frames

In this task you will be asked to look at how frames are used in Desktop Publishing. Open the 'Working with frames' worksheet on the website and follow the instructions.

Putting it all together

To create the design that we made in Unit 2.4 for the nuclear power article, we need several frames.

Figure 1 Layout for an article about nuclear power

One WordArt frame for the title. It has a black background with white text.

Three more text frames for the main text. These are in columns. We will be using text flow so that the text automatically flows from one frame to the next.

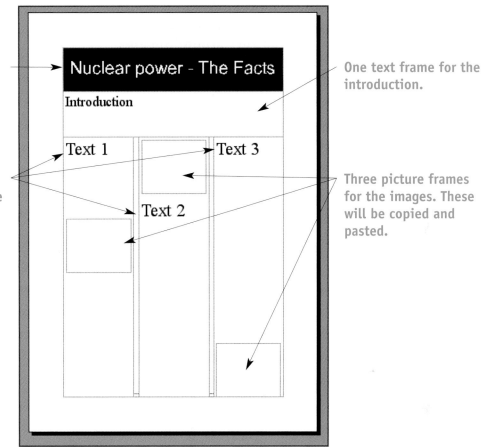

One text frame for the introduction.

Three picture frames for the images. These will be copied and pasted.

Skills Tutorial 2

This tutorial shows you how to get text to flow from one frame to another.

Text flow

This article uses three columns of text, labelled Text 1, Text 2 and Text 3. We need the text to flow from Text 1 to Text 2 and then to Text 3. You do this using the text flow option to link the frames together. If there is too much text to fit into the first text box, it flows into the second text box, and so on.

Once you have added the frames you can start to put the information into the magazine article.

End of Unit Activity: Creating a magazine article

In this activity you will be asked to create a magazine article. Open the 'Creating a magazine article' worksheet on the website and follow the instructions.

2.6 | Working with text and images in DTP software

In this unit you will learn how to:
> **Layer frames on top of each other**
> **Wrap text around images**
> **Crop images**
> **Rotate images and text**

Introduction

There are some features of desktop publishing (DTP) that can help you to create different effects with your publication. If you use these effects appropriately, they can add impact to your publications. Before you use them, you should think about whether they are suitable for the *purpose* and the *audience*.

Many of these effects are to do with the way that the text and images are used. Look at the two publications below. They are both for a poster advertising a birthday party. Can you spot the differences?

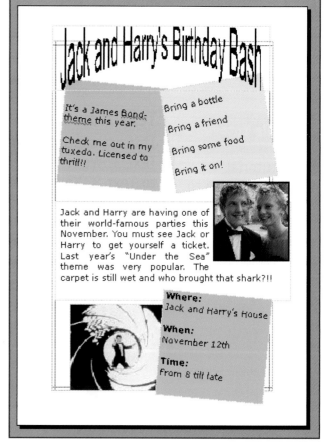

Figure 1 Spot the differences

Layering frames

DTP uses frames. So far we have made sure that the frames are all separated, but we can overlap the frames to create different effects. For example, the poster on the right in Figure 1 has overlapped the frames so that some appear on top of others.

 **Skills Tutorial 1** | This tutorial shows you how to layer frames.

Figure 2 'Wrapping' text

Wrapping text

Text wrapping is when the text automatically goes onto a new line. Usually this happens at the end of every line. You can set it so that the text wraps around the images in the same way as the block of text in the middle of the poster on the right in Figure 1.

 **Skills Tutorial 2** | This tutorial shows you how to wrap text around an image.

Cropping images

You can 'crop' images, which means that you can get rid of parts of it to focus in on the main image. For example, the image on the left in Figure 3 shows a picture of Jack and Harry. The house in the background is not really needed. The image on the right has the house cropped out. You might also have noticed that the photo on the left has been distorted (the people look squashed). This has been put right in the photo on the right.

 Skills Tutorial 3 | This tutorial shows you how to crop images.

Figure 3 Spot the differences

Rotating images

You can also rotate text and images, which means that you can turn them. This has been done with the coloured text boxes in the poster on the right in Figure 1. If you rotate a text box, you have to make sure that people will still be able to read the text. If you rotate an image, make sure it is still clear what the image is showing.

Skills Tutorial 4 | This tutorial shows you how to rotate images.

Written Task: Improving the layout

In this task you will be asked to suggest improvements to the design and layout of an advert. Open the 'Improving the layout' worksheet on the website and follow the instructions.

Figure 4 First version of the car advert

For sale

Call Tony on 07970 555555 for more details.

Only £500 ono

VW Golf Estate

Red
140,000 miles
6 months tax
6 months MOT
Full service history

This is a lovely little run-around. It's in really good condition for the year and has only had three owners. It has a full service history and is a very reliable car. It's got a roof rack and a towbar and is an ideal car for towing a caravan or trailer.

 End of Unit Activity: Changing the magazine article

In this activity you will be asked to make improvements to a magazine article and explain what you have done. Open the 'Changing the magazine article' worksheet on the website and follow the instructions.

 End of Module Assignment: Creating an advert

In this assignment you will be asked to create an A5 colour advert for a new music TV station. Open the 'Module 2 assignment' worksheet on the website and follow the instructions.

········· ## Case Study introduction

Figure 1 Shaheen in her shop

Q What might be the differences between a computer system set up for gaming compared to one set up for a business to use? Think about the different hardware that might be needed.

This is Shaheen. She runs a computer shop in town. Shaheen sells customised computer systems. This means that she sells the computer tower, or desktop, and all the other hardware that goes with it. Customers can pick and choose what hardware they want. Shaheen then uses her own computer to work out the total price. Some customers want very expensive systems that they can use for gaming. Others are business people who need to create and print lots of documents.

Customers usually spend some time with Shaheen working out the best options. Most customers have a certain amount of money to spend, so it is useful if Shaheen can tell them how much the different options will cost.

Earl has come into the shop to buy a new gaming system. He wants to buy a powerful computer that will run the latest PC games. He also wants to play online. He wants:

> an XPZ7000 Tower at £600
> a 19-inch flat screen at £150
> a DVD drive at £50
> a high-speed modem at £50
> speakers at £40.

Figure 2 Shaheen's initial spreadsheet

Q Earl has got £800 to spend. How can Shaheen work out if he has got enough money? What if he hasn't got enough? What methods could Shaheen use to help her work out the prices of these different options?

Earl goes home to think about all the options. Shaheen decides to set up a spreadsheet model to help her (Figure 2). Shaheen spends some time setting up the spreadsheet. She uses a formula to add up the total price of all the items. She includes a cell where she can type in how much the customer has got to spend and adds another formula to work out whether the customer has got enough money. Finally she adds a title and some text labels and formats the spreadsheet to make it clear and easy to use (Figure 3).

Q What does Shaheen need to do to this spreadsheet model so that it is ready to use?

Figure 3 Spreadsheet modified to calculate amounts

Figure 4 Spreadsheet with a cheaper tower

	A	B	C
1	**Computer price model**		
2			
3	**Item**	**Price**	
4	XPZ6500 Tower	£ 550.00	
5	19-inch flat screen	£ 150.00	
6	DVD drive	£ 50.00	
7	High speed modem	£ 50.00	
8	Speakers	£ 40.00	
9			
10	**Total**	£ 840.00	
11	Amount customer has to spend	£ 800.00	
12	Amount left	-£ 40.00	

The following day, Earl comes back. He's forgotten most of the options and is still confused. Shaheen opens up her spreadsheet model. They can now work through the options together.

Earl's first choice (Figure 3) gives an 'amount left' value of minus £90, which means that Earl needs another £90 to be able to afford these items. They try entering a cheaper tower, the XPZ6500 at £550 (Figure 4).

Earl is still £40 short. Finally they try the cheapest tower, the XPZ6000 at £500 (Figure 5). Earl can afford this computer system and still have £10 left over.

Another customer comes into the shop. She is a business woman. She wants a computer system that she can use to write business letters and print them out. She also wants to use her computer for emailing.

> **Q** How can Shaheen use the spreadsheet model to help her with the new customer? What changes might she need to make to her spreadsheet model?

Figure 5 Spreadsheet with the cheapest tower

	A	B	C
1	**Computer price model**		
2			
3	**Item**	**Price**	
4	XPZ6000 Tower	£ 500.00	
5	19-inch flat screen	£ 150.00	
6	DVD drive	£ 50.00	
7	High speed modem	£ 50.00	
8	Speakers	£ 40.00	
9			
10	**Total**	£ 790.00	
11	Amount customer has to spend	£ 800.00	
12	Amount left	£ 10.00	

Figure 6 Spreadsheet of Shaheen's annual sales

File Edit View Insert Format Tools Data FlashPaper Window Help

140% Arial

E17

	A	B	C	D
1	Shaheen Computers Annual Sales			
2				
3	Month	Number of systems sold	Money made	
4	January	5	£ 5,200.00	
5	February	7	£ 8,400.00	
6	March	10	£ 11,984.00	
7	April	12	£ 13,546.00	
8	May	8	£ 9,768.00	
9	June	5	£ 5,647.00	
10	July	6	£ 6,574.00	
11	August	4	£ 4,563.00	
12	September	9	£ 9,876.00	
13	October	10	£ 10,986.00	
14	November	15	£ 16,758.00	
15	December	18	£ 18,765.00	
16				
17	Total	109	£ 122,067.00	

Q How else could Shaheen present this information to make it easier to read?

Shaheen's business has had a good year. She thinks that using the model has really helped her to provide a good service to customers. She uses another spreadsheet model to keep track of how many computer systems she has sold and how much money she has made this year.

The spreadsheet is quite detailed and shows all the figures.

Shaheen decides to create a graph of the information. Once she has done this it is much easier to see the pattern.

For example, it seems that December is a really good month for Shaheen, while things are not so good in the summer months.

Figure 7 Graph of Shaheen's annual sales

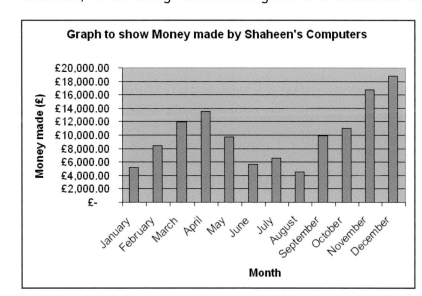

3.1 Working with spreadsheet models

Learning Objectives

In this unit you will learn:

> **What a spreadsheet model is**
> **The basics of how spreadsheet models work**
> **How to answer 'what if' questions using a spreadsheet model**

Introduction to spreadsheets

Spreadsheet software is used when you need to work with numbers and calculations. It contains different types of calculation, called 'formulae'. You can use these to set up spreadsheet models. A model is where you recreate a real life situation on your computer. You can use a model to ask 'what if' type questions and then see what happens.

A spreadsheet is a grid made up of 'columns' and 'rows'. Each column is given a letter and each row is given a number. Where a column and a row meet is called a 'cell'.

Below is a simple spreadsheet model that Pete uses in his paintball store to work out how much it costs to buy different items.

The columns are vertical. Column D is highlighted here.

The rows are horizontal. Row 4 is highlighted here.

The cell is where the column and row meet. Cell D4 is highlighted here.

Figure 1 Spreadsheets have columns, rows and cells

Entering information into a spreadsheet

Cells are very important in spreadsheets as everything you type into a spreadsheet is put into a cell. You need to get used to the idea of identifying each cell using its 'cell reference', e.g. A1, D4, etc. The column letter is first, followed by the row number.

There are only three things that you can type into the cell of a spreadsheet:

> Text: used for headings and labels
> Numbers: used for typing in values
> Formulae: these are calculations carried out on the numbers you have typed in.

Using formulae is really important because it means that the spreadsheet will do all the calculations automatically. If you change any of the numbers in the spreadsheet, the formulae will automatically re-do the calculations for you. When you make your own spreadsheet, you should use a formula whenever you can.

 Written Task: The computer shop model

In this task you will be asked to answer questions about a spreadsheet model used by a computer shop. Open the 'The computer shop model' worksheet on the website and follow the instructions.

Figure 2 Paintballing

Using a spreadsheet

Pete already has his spreadsheet set up and he can use it every time someone buys something from his store. All he has to do is type in the name of the products they have bought in column A and the price and quantity of each product in the next two columns. The spreadsheet does the rest for him, as shown on page 44. He can now do some of the 'what if' type questions mentioned earlier.

For example:

> What if someone buys three lots of paintballs? Pete would type '3' into cell C8 and then the spreadsheet would update automatically to show the new 'total price'.
> What if the price of the paintball gun was £139.99? Pete would change the value in cell B4 to £139.99.

You are now going to use a spreadsheet model to carry out some 'what if' questions of your own.

 End of Unit Activity: The skateboard model

In this activity you will be asked to use a spreadsheet model to answer questions. Open the 'The skateboard model' worksheet on the website and follow the instructions.

3.2 | Refining a model

In this unit you will learn:
> How a model is based on rules
> How formulae are used in spreadsheet models
> How to enter formulae

The rules of a model

In Unit 3.1, we looked at the spreadsheet model used by Pete in his paintball store. He uses the model to work out how much it would cost to buy different combinations of products.

All models have rules that explain how the model works:

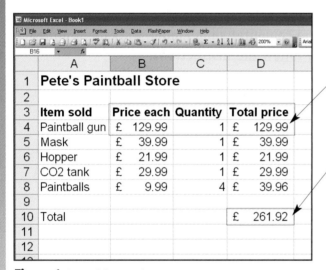

Rule 1: The 'total price' in column D is calculated like this:
'price each' x 'quantity'.

Rule 2 : The 'total' amount shown in cell D10 is calculated by adding up all of the prices shown in column D.

Figure 1 Spreadsheet rules

Each rule is added to the model using a formula. This means that the values are calculated automatically.

Entering the rules

Let's look at how two of the formulae have been added to the model.

Rule 1

In cell D4, the value of £129.99 is shown. This has been worked out using a formula. Remember that a formula is simply a bit of maths. The calculation needed here is the value in cell B4 multiplied by the value in cell C4. The answer is then shown in D4.

In a spreadsheet, you click on cell D4 and then type: =B4*C4

The equals sign (=) means that it is a formula and the * sign means that it will multiply the values in the two cells.

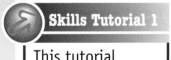
Skills Tutorial 1

This tutorial shows you how to enter formulae.

Rule 2

In cell D10, the value £261.92 is shown. This has also been worked out using a formula. The calculation needed is to add up all the values in cells D4, D5, D6, D7 and D8.

In a spreadsheet you would click on cell D10 and type:
=D4+D5+D6+D7+D8

Notice that all formulae MUST start with the equals sign (=).

Written Task: Phone bill model

In this task you will be asked questions about the rules of a spreadsheet model. Open the 'Phone bill model' worksheet on the website and follow the instructions.

Changing the rules

If you change the rules in a model, you will have to change the formulae or add new formulae. We are going to add a new rule to Pete's paintball store model. Pete sometimes sends items by post. The new rule is that £10 needs to be added to the total price to cover postage. The model now looks like the one shown in Figure 2.

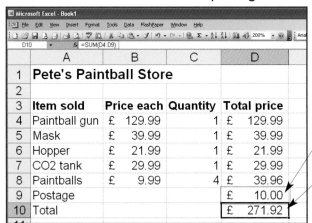

The postage cost has been added in Row 9. The £10 postage cost has been put in cell D9.

The formula in cell D10 has been changed so that it includes the £10. The new formula is: =SUM (D4:D9).

Figure 2 Spreadsheet with new rule

Skills Tutorial 2

This tutorial shows you how to insert new rows and columns and change formulae.

Practical Task: Extending the model

In this task you will be asked to make changes to a spreadsheet model. Open the 'Extending the model' worksheet on the website and follow the instructions.

End of Unit Activity: Redball Bowling

In this activity you will be asked to complete a spreadsheet model and then answer questions using the model. Open the 'Redball Bowling' worksheet on the website and follow the instructions.

3.3 | Creating a simple model

In this unit you will learn how to:
> **Create a spreadsheet model**
> **Enter text, numbers and formulae**
> **Test that your model works**

Simple models

Designing the model

In Units 3.1 and 3.2, we used spreadsheet models that had already been set up. In this unit, we will be setting up a spreadsheet model from scratch.

Clancy's Computer Shop wants to use a spreadsheet model to work out how many different items it sells each month, and how much money it makes. They sell these items:

> Desktops for £399.99
> Screens for £129.99
> DVD drives for £29.99
> Speakers for £19.99
> Printers for £79.99.

This month they have sold 30 desktops, 30 screens, 10 DVD drives, 10 speakers and 5 printers.

The first stage of creating a model is to work out what text, numbers and formulae are needed to solve the problem and to create a design. It is a good idea to plan this on paper first.

Figure 1 Sketch for spreadsheet model

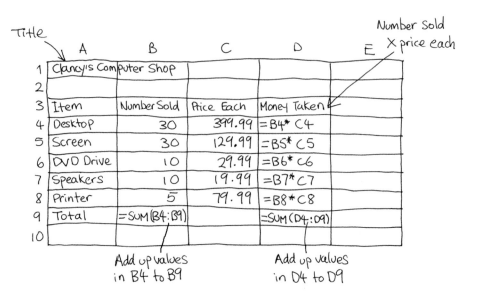

Written Task: Jane's bicycle

In this task you will be asked to create a hand-drawn design for a spreadsheet model. Open the 'Jane's bicycle' worksheet on the website and follow the instructions.

Creating the model

You are now ready to start using the spreadsheet software. In this unit, we will look at how to get the basics right, and make sure that we set up the formulae correctly. We will sort out the layout in Unit 3.4.

Start by typing in the text, then the values shown above for Clancy's shop. Your spreadsheet should look like this:

Figure 2 Clancy's first spreadsheet

	A	B	C	D
1	Clancy's Computer Shop			
2				
3	Item	Number sold	Price each	Money taken
4	Desktop	30	399.99	
5	Screen	30	129.99	
6	DVD drive	10	29.99	
7	Speakers	10	19.99	
8	Printer	5	79.99	
9				

You will need to make columns B, C and D a bit wider so that the text fits in neatly.

Figure 3 Clancy's Computer Shop

Skills Tutorial 1 | This tutorial shows you how to add text and numbers and change the width of columns.

Creating formulae

Cells D4 to D8 are blank at the moment and they need formulae in them. When trying to work out the formula, it is perhaps easier to forget about the fact that you are using a spreadsheet and just think about it logically. For example, in cell D4, the shop has sold 30 desktops for £399.99 each, so that's 30 x 399.99. As a formulae this is: =B4*C4.

A similar formula is needed in cells D5 to D8, so you can now copy this formula into cells D5 to D8.

There are two other useful totals we could add here:

> We could add up the total number sold in column B and put it in cell B9.
> We could add up the total money taken in column D and put it in cell D9.

You can do this using the SUM formula you were shown in Unit 3.2 or using the autosum option. Your finished spreadsheet should now look like this:

Figure 4 Clancy's finished spreadsheet

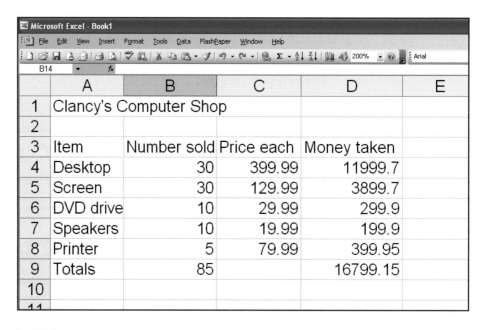

	A	B	C	D	E
1	Clancy's Computer Shop				
2					
3	Item	Number sold	Price each	Money taken	
4	Desktop	30	399.99	11999.7	
5	Screen	30	129.99	3899.7	
6	DVD drive	10	29.99	299.9	
7	Speakers	10	19.99	199.9	
8	Printer	5	79.99	399.95	
9	Totals	85		16799.15	
10					
11					

Skills Tutorial 2 | This tutorial shows you how to add formulae.

Testing the formulae

Whenever you use a formula, it is always worth testing it to make sure you have done it properly. There are three ways that you could do this:

> Check that the answers are roughly what you would expect. For example, in B9, you could check (in your head) that the values in B4 to B8 add up to 85.
> Get your calculator out and check them. For example, you could check that the value in D9 is correct by checking that 30 x 399.99 is 11,999.7
> Change some of the numbers and check that the calculated values change. For example, change the '30' in cell B5 to '40' and see what happens in cell D4. It should go up.

Figure 5 Inside Clancy's Computer Shop

End of Unit Activity: Inks R Us

In this activity you will be asked to design, create and test a spreadsheet model. Open the 'Inks R Us' worksheet on the website and follow the instructions.

3.4 Formatting and labelling a model

Learning Objectives

In this unit you will learn how to:

- **Create a suitable layout for a spreadsheet model**
- **Format text**
- **Format numbers**
- **Format cells**

Formatting and labelling spreadsheet models

Creating a suitable layout

In Unit 3.3 we created a spreadsheet model for Clancy's Computer Shop. By the time we had finished, it looked like Figure 1:

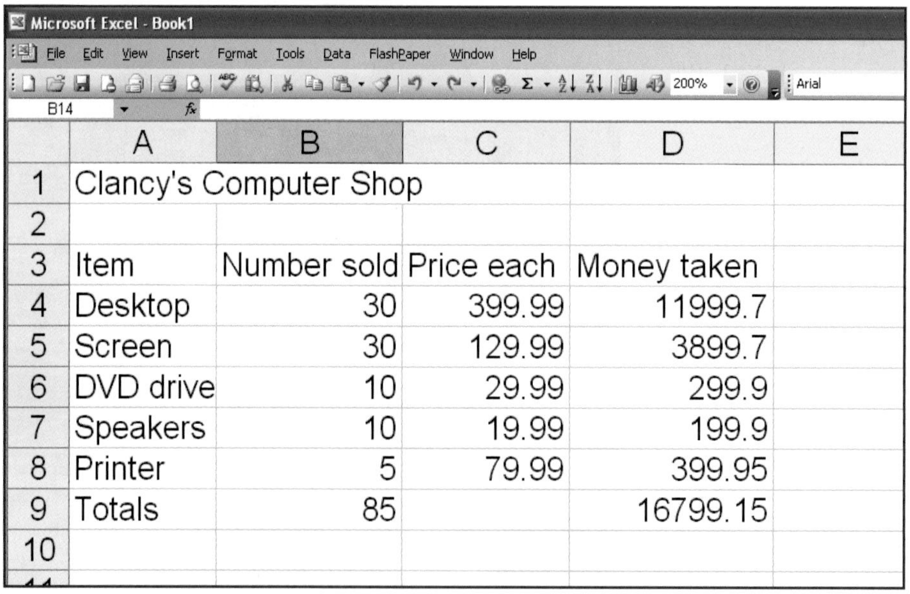

	A	B	C	D	E
1	Clancy's Computer Shop				
2					
3	Item	Number sold	Price each	Money taken	
4	Desktop	30	399.99	11999.7	
5	Screen	30	129.99	3899.7	
6	DVD drive	10	29.99	299.9	
7	Speakers	10	19.99	199.9	
8	Printer	5	79.99	399.95	
9	Totals	85		16799.15	
10					

Figure 1 Clancy's finished spreadsheet

The spreadsheet model has some basic formatting and labelling:

- The model has a title in row 1: Clancy's Computer Shop.
- We left row 2 blank to break up the information and make it easier to read.
- We used row 3 to type in text labels that explain what is in each column. We have four columns of information: Item, Number sold, Price each and Money taken.
- We made some of the columns wider to fit the text labels in.

There are other things that we could do to the spreadsheet model to improve the layout and make it easier to read:

> The numbers in columns C and D should be formatted so that they show as currency, e.g. £399.99 instead of 399.99.
> The title (row 1) and text labels (row 3) would be better if they stood out a bit more.
> The totals in row 9 are quite important and they need to stand out more.

If you were making a PowerPoint presentation or a brochure, you would spend a lot of time on the layout. You should do the same thing with a spreadsheet model.

Written Task: Arches Garage

In this task you will be asked to suggest improvements to the layout of a spreadsheet model. Open the 'Arches garage' worksheet on the website and follow the instructions.

Formatting text

Text can be formatted in a spreadsheet model in the same ways that it can in other software, for example, Microsoft Word. This means that you can use the following techniques:

> make the text larger or smaller
> change the font style
> use italics, bold or underline
> change the text colour.

You need to think carefully about how you use these options. The person using the spreadsheet needs to be able to read the information clearly. If you use too many different techniques, you might actually make it harder for them to read.

 This tutorial shows you how to format text.

Formatting numbers

Numbers can have many different formats. For example:

> Currency is shown like this: £199.99
> Dates are shown like this: 25/12/2007
> Whole numbers are shown like this: 35
> Decimals (to 2 decimal places) are shown like this: 35.32
> Time is shown like this: 12:02pm
> Percentages are shown like this: 73%.

You must format the numbers in the cells so that they are suitable. In this spreadsheet model, the numbers in columns C and D need changing to a currency format.

You can also use the text formatting options on numbers. For example, you can change the font style of the numbers, as well as the size and colour.

 **Skills Tutorial 2** See how you can format numbers to currency, and also learn about some of the other number formats.

Formatting cells

You can also format the actual cells themselves. There are two main techniques:

> fill the cell with colour
> put a border around the cell.

These options are really useful for making information stand out. Again, you need to be careful how you use them. For example, if you put blue text on a blue background, it would be very difficult to read.

 **Skills Tutorial 3** This tutorial shows you how to use borders and shading.

Putting it all together

When you design the layout and format of a spreadsheet model, you do need to think about how you will combine all of these different techniques. You need to think about who will be using the spreadsheet model and what they will be using it for.

For example, Clancy's Computer Shop model is being used for a business. The layout needs to be very clear so that Clancy can read the information easily. It does not really need to have lots of font styles and colours, but the main information does need to stand out. Look at the examples in Figures 2 and 3.

 Written Task: Putting it all together

In this task you will be asked to compare the layout of two spreadsheet models. Open the 'Putting it all together' worksheet on the website and follow the instructions.

Figure 2 Clancy's Computer Shop model: format 1

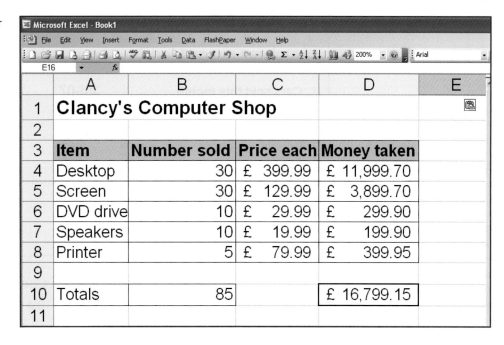

Figure 3 Clancy's Computer Shop model: format 2

Which one is the easiest to read? Which two changes are the most important? Check with one of your classmates. What do they think?

End of Unit Activity: Inks R Us formatting

In this activity you will be asked to improve the layout of the Inks R Us spreadsheet model and explain your improvements. Open the 'Inks R Us formatting' worksheet on the website and follow the instructions.

3.5 | Developing a model

Making the model more realistic

In Unit 3.4, we looked at the Arches Garage spreadsheet model. Phil, the owner, uses it to work out how much money he gets from selling cars.

Figure 1 Arches Garage model

	A	B	E	F
1	Arches Garage Model			
2				
3	**Cars sold this month**		**Jul-07**	
4				
5	**Make**	**Price of car**	**Year**	
6	Ford Ka	£ 1,550.00	1999	
7	Renault Clio	£ 1,200.00	1998	
8	Citroen Xantia	£ 900.00	1997	
9	Ford Focus	£ 3,500.00	2001	
10	Vauxhall Astra	£ 3,800.00	2003	
11				
12	Total	£ 10,950.00		

The problem with this model is that it is not very realistic. Phil has got £10,950 from selling cars (as shown in B12), but he will have had to pay for the cars in the first place. For example, he might have sold the Ford Ka for £1550 but he will have had to buy it from someone else first. If he paid £1000 for it, then he has only actually made £550 on it. This is called *profit*.

Price of car − Cost of car = Profit
£1550.00 − £1000.00 = £550

Written Task: Calculating profit

In this task you will be asked to use a spreadsheet model to calculate profit. Open the 'Calculating profit' worksheet on the website and follow the instructions.

Extending the model

Phil needs to add the profit calculation into his spreadsheet model. He could do it like this:

Figure 2 Phil can see his profit

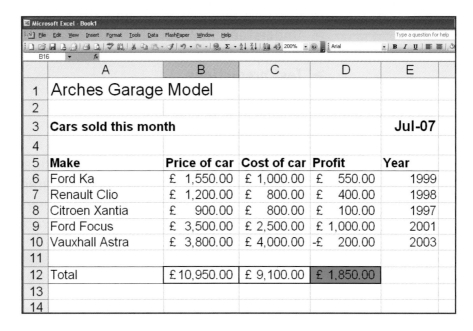

Let's look at what he has done:

> He has changed the text label in B5 to read 'Price of car' (this is how much Phil *sells* each car for).
> He has inserted a new column C and used this for the cost of the car (this is how much Phil *bought* each car for).
> He has inserted a new column D and used this to work out the profit (Price of car – Cost of car).
> He has added up the total profit in D12 and coloured the cell green to make it stand out.

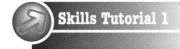

Skills Tutorial 1 | This tutorial shows you how to calculate profit.

End of Unit Activity: MeBay sales

In this activity you will be asked to develop a spreadsheet model and use it to answer questions. Open the 'MeBay sales' worksheet on the website and follow the instructions.

3.6 | Making and testing predictions

In this unit you will learn how to:
> **Understand how variables are related to each other**
> **Make predictions**
> **Test predictions**

············ # Introduction

In Unit 3.5, we looked at profit. We calculated it using a formula, which was Price – Cost. In the Arches Garage model, it is useful for Phil so that he knows whether his business is making any profit. For example, in July he made a profit of £1850.

Figure 1 Arches Garage model

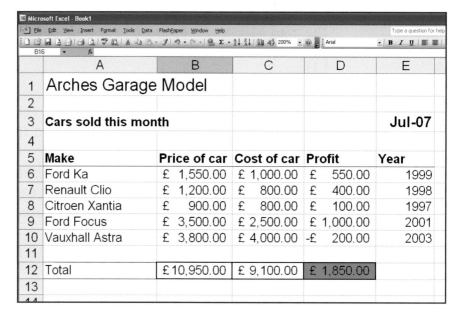

But how else could Phil use this spreadsheet model? He could use it to answer questions like this:

> What if I sell the Renault Clio for £1300?
> What if I sell the Ford Ka for £900?
> What if I bought the Ford Focus for £3500?
> What if I sell the Vauxhall Astra for £4000?
> What if I want to make more profit?

Written Task: Gita's Guitars

In this task you will be asked to work out the rules of a spreadsheet model. Open the 'Gita's Guitars' worksheet on the website and follow the instructions.

Making predictions

It is possible to predict what will happen if any of the values change in the spreadsheet. If Phil sold the Renault Clio for £1300:

> The value in B7 would go up from at £1200 to £1300.
> The value in C7 would stay the same at £800.
> The value in D7 would change because it is calculated using the formula =B7-C7. This would go up from £400 to £500.
> The value in D12 would also change because it is calculated using the formula =SUM(D6:D10). This would go up from £1850 to £1950.
> The value in B12 would change because it is calculated using the formula =SUM(B6:B10). This would go up from £10,950 to £11,050.

Figure 2 Arches Garage

So, a small change in the price of one of the cars has caused three other values to change.

This shows that if Phil puts the price of his cars up he will make more profit. The problem is that in real life, lots of things might change at the same time. For example, Phil might put the price of the car up, but he might have to pay more for it when he buys it. This means that the price and the cost both go up at the same time. What effect will that have on profit?

Testing predictions

The good thing about a spreadsheet model is that you can try out all of these 'what if' questions to see what will happen. Phil can type in the various numbers and have a look at what will happen to his profit.

Phil buys some new cars at the end of July, but August is a bad month for Phil. No one is buying his cars, so he decides to see what might happen if he reduces the price.

Figure 3 Phil has some bad predictions for August

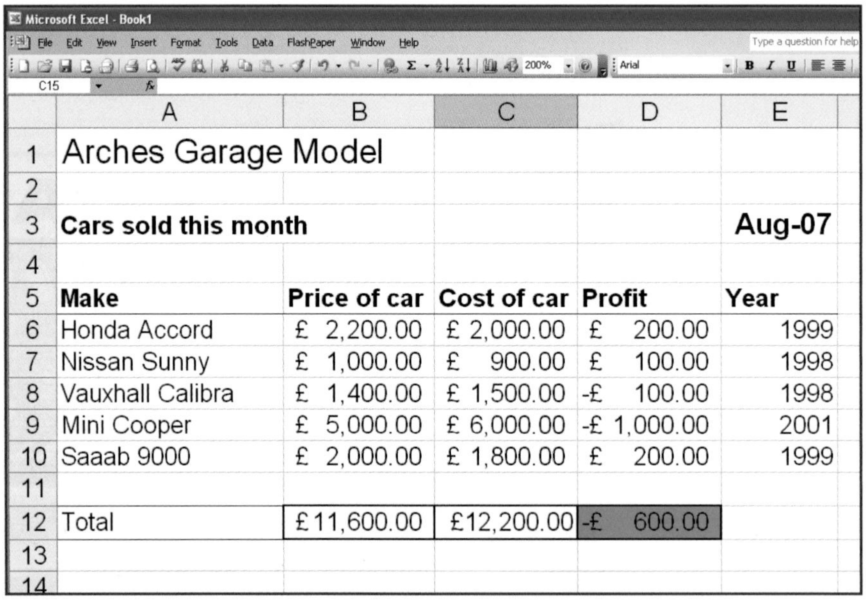

	A	B	C	D	E
1	Arches Garage Model				
2					
3	**Cars sold this month**				**Aug-07**
4					
5	**Make**	**Price of car**	**Cost of car**	**Profit**	**Year**
6	Honda Accord	£ 2,200.00	£ 2,000.00	£ 200.00	1999
7	Nissan Sunny	£ 1,000.00	£ 900.00	£ 100.00	1998
8	Vauxhall Calibra	£ 1,400.00	£ 1,500.00	-£ 100.00	1998
9	Mini Cooper	£ 5,000.00	£ 6,000.00	-£ 1,000.00	2001
10	Saaab 9000	£ 2,000.00	£ 1,800.00	£ 200.00	1999
11					
12	Total	£11,600.00	£12,200.00	-£ 600.00	
13					
14					

He tries these prices because if the cars are cheap, he knows someone will buy them. He can see from this that he has set the prices too low as the total profit figure is -£600. This means that he would not make any profit at all; in fact he would make a loss.

Phil can now play around with the price figures until he is happy that he can sell his cars and still make a profit.

Figure 4 Inside Phil's car showroom

 End of Unit Activity: Julie's Jewellery

In this activity you will be asked to use a spreadsheet model to make and test predictions. Open the 'Julie's Jewellery' document on the website and follow the instructions.

Figure 5 Julie's Jewellery model

	A	B	C	D
1	**Julie's Jewellery Shop**			
2				
3	Item	Price	Cost	Profit
4	Gold chain	£ 250.00	£ 200.00	£ 50.00
5	Necklace	£ 130.00	£ 120.00	£ 10.00
6	Bracelet	£ 95.00	£ 60.00	£ 35.00
7	Earrings	£ 85.00	£ 60.00	£ 25.00
8	Ring	£ 150.00	£ 90.00	£ 60.00
9				
10	Total	£ 710.00	£ 530.00	£ 180.00
11				

3.7 Creating a graph

Learning Objectives	In this unit you will learn how to:

> Create appropriate graphs from a spreadsheet model
> Select what data to plot
> Select what type of graph to use
> Label the graph appropriately

Using graphs

Figure 1 Arches Garage: Annual Sales

	A	B	C	D	E
1	Arches Garage Annual Sales				
2					
3	Month	Number of cars sold	Total cost of cars	Total sales	Total profit
4	January	8	£ 12,546.00	£ 16,152.00	£ 3,606.00
5	February	6	£ 13,456.00	£ 14,543.00	£ 1,087.00
6	March	10	£ 17,654.00	£ 21,765.00	£ 4,111.00
7	April	14	£ 22,490.00	£ 25,765.00	£ 3,275.00
8	May	20	£ 28,976.00	£ 32,876.00	£ 3,900.00
9	June	12	£ 19,804.00	£ 23,452.00	£ 3,648.00
10	July	9	£ 15,876.00	£ 17,543.00	£ 1,667.00
11	August	6	£ 12,998.00	£ 14,322.00	£ 1,324.00
12	September	5	£ 10,692.00	£ 12,944.00	£ 2,252.00
13	October	6	£ 10,657.00	£ 13,946.00	£ 3,289.00
14	November	4	£ 2,500.00	£ 4,500.00	£ 2,000.00
15	December	3	£ 2,300.00	£ 3,678.00	£ 1,378.00
16					
17	Totals	103	£169,949.00	£201,486.00	£31,537.00
18					

Graphs are a useful way of presenting numerical information. For example, earlier on we came across Phil at the Arches Garage. He used a spreadsheet model to keep track of how many cars he sold each month. He could set up another spreadsheet to keep track of this over the whole year.

As you can see, the spreadsheet model looks quite complicated and it is difficult to read all of the information. If Phil wanted to know how many cars he had sold each month, he might find it easier to create a graph like the one in Figure 2.

Figure 2 A graph makes it easier to see the trends

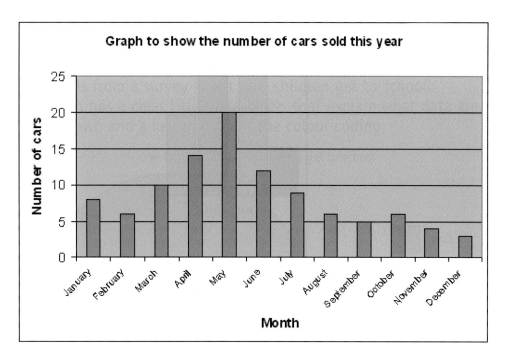

You can see that it is now much easier for Phil to keep track of the sale of cars over the month. For example, which month did Phil sell the most cars? Which was his worst month?

Selecting the data and the graph type

You need to think carefully about the data that you want to plot and the style of graph that you use. The basic rule is that your graph should make the information easier to understand.

 Written Task: Graph examples

In this task you will be asked to decide what types of graph to use. Open the 'Graph examples' worksheet on the website and follow the instructions.

Figure 3 Graph examples from the Written Task

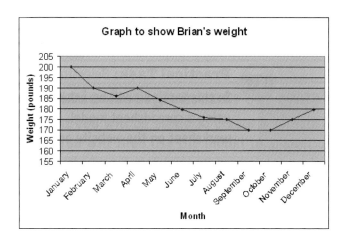

4 | DATA HANDLING

Case Study introduction

Figure 1 Mussie and Ellie

Mussie and Ellie are school friends. They get on well together, but sometimes they disagree about things. They have just finished their RE lesson. The teacher had been talking about charities and how school children do not do as much for charity as adults. Mussie thinks his teacher is probably right, but Ellie is not so sure.

> **Q** How could Mussie and Ellie find out whether older people do more for charity than younger people?

At break-time, Mussie and Ellie go off to the computer room. They decide to go on the Internet to see if they can find some information to help them. They look at some charity websites, and do some searches to see if they can find the information they need. After a while, they find some information from one children's charity on how much money different age groups give to the charity each year.

Figure 2 Kids Care International

Age group	Donations in 2003	Donations in 2004	Donations in 2005	Donations in 2006
0 - 18	£ 1,200.00	£ 1,420.00	£ 1,642.00	£ 1,845.00
19 and over	£ 3,200.00	£ 2,783.00	£ 2,634.00	£ 2,341.00

Donations to KidsCare International

Figure 2 A graph makes it easier to see the trends

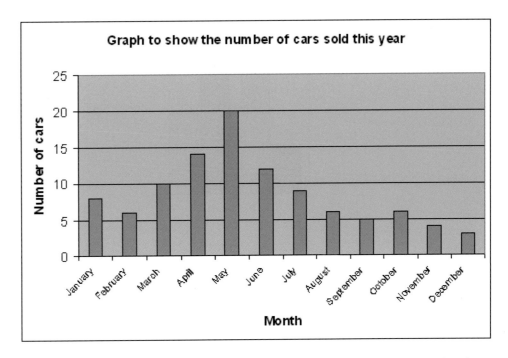

You can see that it is now much easier for Phil to keep track of the sale of cars over the month. For example, which month did Phil sell the most cars? Which was his worst month?

Selecting the data and the graph type

You need to think carefully about the data that you want to plot and the style of graph that you use. The basic rule is that your graph should make the information easier to understand.

 Written Task: Graph examples

In this task you will be asked to decide what types of graph to use. Open the 'Graph examples' worksheet on the website and follow the instructions.

Figure 3 Graph examples from the Written Task

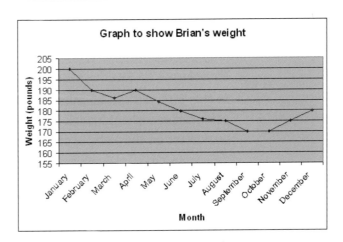

Figure 3 Types of graph

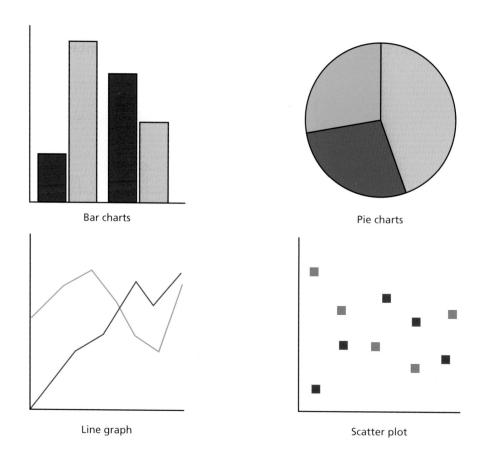

Bar charts

Pie charts

Line graph

Scatter plot

There are many different types of graph. The main ones are shown in Figure 3.

For example, if you are showing information spread over a period of time, a bar chart or line graph would be most suitable. If you are showing information where you wanted to plot percentages, a pie chart might be better. If you are plotting the results of a science experiment, a scatter plot might be best.

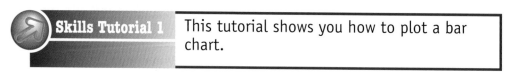

Skills Tutorial 1   This tutorial shows you how to plot a bar chart.

Practical Task: Selecting graph types

In this task you will be asked to create suitable graphs using a spreadsheet model. Open the 'Selecting graph types' worksheet on the website and follow the instructions.

Labelling the graph

It is very important to add a clear title and axis labels to your graph. Some graphs might need a key as well. The example in Figure 4 is from a survey about how children get to school. The graph has a clear title, data labels that explain what data are being shown and a key to explain the colour coding.

Figure 4 Pie charts compare percentages clearly

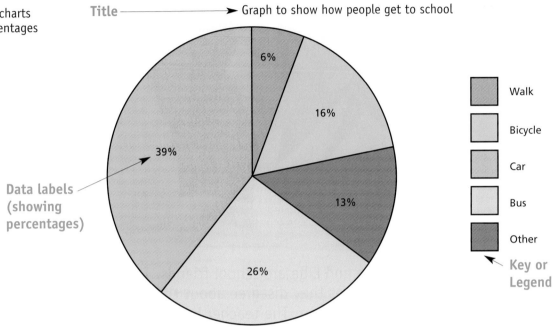

Title ──────────► Graph to show how people get to school

Data labels (showing percentages)

Key or Legend

Walk
Bicycle
Car
Bus
Other

Skills Tutorial 2 This tutorial shows you how to plot a pie chart.

 End of Unit Activity: Creating graphs

In this activity you will be asked to create graphs and explain what types of graphs you have used. Open the 'Creating graphs' worksheet on the website and follow the instructions.

 End of Module Assignment: Car rentals

In this assignment you will be asked to create a spreadsheet model for a car rental company. You will then use the model to answer questions and create graphs. Open the 'Module 3 assignment' worksheet on the website and follow the instructions.

Case Study introduction

Figure 1 Mussie and Ellie

Mussie and Ellie are school friends. They get on well together, but sometimes they disagree about things. They have just finished their RE lesson. The teacher had been talking about charities and how school children do not do as much for charity as adults. Mussie thinks his teacher is probably right, but Ellie is not so sure.

> **Q** How could Mussie and Ellie find out whether older people do more for charity than younger people?

At break-time, Mussie and Ellie go off to the computer room. They decide to go on the Internet to see if they can find some information to help them. They look at some charity websites, and do some searches to see if they can find the information they need. After a while, they find some information from one children's charity on how much money different age groups give to the charity each year.

Figure 2 Kids Care International

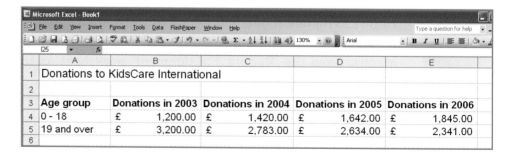

Age group	Donations in 2003	Donations in 2004	Donations in 2005	Donations in 2006
0 - 18	£ 1,200.00	£ 1,420.00	£ 1,642.00	£ 1,845.00
19 and over	£ 3,200.00	£ 2,783.00	£ 2,634.00	£ 2,341.00

Mussie is happy because he thinks it proves him right.

> **Q** Why does Mussie think that these data prove him right? Why might Ellie think that these data do not prove him right?

Mussie explains to Ellie that if she looks at the numbers, it shows that the amount of money donated by older people is more than the amount donated by younger people. This proves that older people do more for charity than school pupils. Ellie is still not sure. She points out to Mussie that:

> > This data is only from one charity and this might not be the case for all charities.
> > The amount of money given by young people is going up every year, while the amount given by older people is going down.
> > It only shows the amount of money that people have given. She thinks that although younger people might not be able to afford to give as much as older people, they might spend more time doing charity events.

Ellie thinks that if this trend carries on, young people will soon be donating more to this charity than older people. They decide to test both hypotheses. They decide to do a questionnaire.

> **Q** What questions should they ask?

Ellie and Mussie think about the questions they want to ask:

1 How old are you?
2 How much money do you give to charity?
3 How much time do you spend doing charity work?

Figure 3 Mussie and Ellie handing out questionnaires

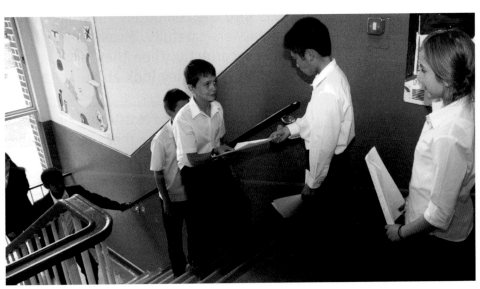

Charity questionnaire

1. How old are you? _____ years

2. Do you donate money to charity? Y/N

3. How much money do you give to charity each month?

£0.00
£0.01 to £10.00
£10.01 to £20.00
£20.01 to £30.00
£30.01 to £40.00
£40.01 or more

4. Do you do charity work? Y/N

5. How much time to spend doing charity work each month?

0 hours
Between 0.1 and 1 hour
Between 1.1 and 2   hours
Between 2.1 and 2   hours
Between 2.1 and 3   hours
3.1 or more hours

6. What type of charity do you donate money to?

Children
Food Aid
Cancer
Medical
Human Rights
Other

If other, please say which _____

7. What type of charity do you give your time to?

Children
Food Aid
Cancer
Medical
Human Rights
Other

Figure 4 The charity questionnaire

They also decide to ask a couple of extra questions to find out about what charities people do give money or time to.

4 What type of charities do you donate money to?
5 What type of charity do you give your time to?
6 What is your favourite charity?

They spend the rest of break making changes to the questions. They spend some time making it look like a proper questionnaire. By the end of break they have finished.

> **Q** How many questionnaires should they hand out? Who do you think should fill in their questionnaire?

Mussie and Ellie decide to print out 30 copies of the questionnaire and hand it out around school. Mussie thinks it would be a good idea to give pupils two copies. This way the pupils can fill in one for themselves and get their parents to fill in one too. They must get older people to fill it in, otherwise the results will be biased towards the pupils.

After the questionnaires have all been filled in, they put all of the answers into the computer. They have to make sure that they type in the answers carefully. Mussie and Ellie know that if data are typed in incorrectly, then they might come to the wrong conclusion when they look at the data later on.

> **Q** Which software could Mussie and Ellie use to put the answers into the computer? How can they check that the data are correct? How could they reduce the number of errors in the data? What problems might there be if the data were typed in incorrectly?

Mussie and Ellie store all of the results in a spreadsheet. This means that they can search and sort the data to find answers to different questions, such as, how many people aged under 18 donate money to charity.

Q What is the best way for Ellie and Mussie to present their results?

Mussie and Ellie decide that they should create a report to show the results. They decide to use a table to show the results of each search. They think that a pie chart will be the best way to show the results of their two hypotheses.

Figure 5 The charts based on the questionnaires

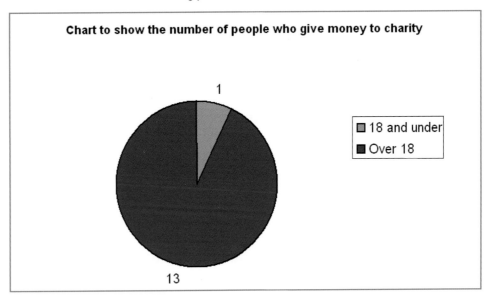

Chart to show the number of people who give money to charity

1

13

◻ 18 and under
■ Over 18

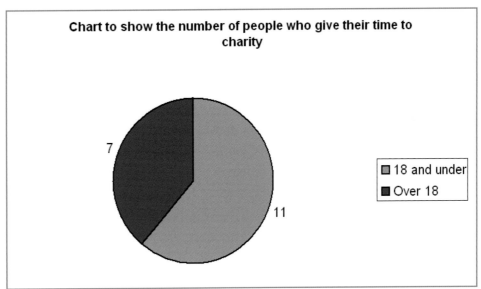

Chart to show the number of people who give their time to charity

7

11

◻ 18 and under
■ Over 18

Going back to the original argument, Mussie thought that adults did more for charity than younger people. If you look at whether they donate to charity or not, then his hypothesis is true. Ellie believed that younger people did more work for charity. Looking at the results, her hypothesis is also true. So in the end they were both right!

4.1 Designing a questionnaire

In this unit you will learn:
> **How questionnaires are used to collect data**
> **How questionnaires can be used to test a hypothesis**
> **How to design an effective questionnaire**
> **How to ask effective questions**

Introduction to questionnaires

A questionnaire is a set of questions that you ask to lots of people. Questionnaires are used to collect data when the data you need is not already available. They are very good for collecting information about people's opinions and attitudes. For example, if we wanted to know what pupils think about their school, we could use a questionnaire to find out this information.

Before you can design a questionnaire you need to know why you are collecting the data and what it is you are trying to find out. You may have a hypothesis that you want to test, such as:

> ICT is more popular than Science
> Year 11 pupils do more homework than Year 7 pupils
> Netball is more popular than basketball.

Written Task: Questions

In this task you will be asked to think of suitable questions to ask for a dating agency questionnaire. Open the 'Questions' worksheet on the website and follow the instructions.

You must then ask the questions that will help you find the answers.

Asking questions

Once you know what you are trying to find out you can start to design your questionnaire. You need to decide:

> what questions to ask
> how to ask effective questions
> how to design the layout to make it easy to fill in.

We are going to design a questionnaire about fashion and find out if girls are more interested in fashion than boys. The questions we ask must be relevant. At the very least we need to ask about gender and their opinion of fashion. We could ask some further questions, for example about age or how much they spend on clothes. This could help gain more detail.

We need to think about the way in which questions are asked and the types of answer that we expect. Look at the two questions below. Both of them seem quite similar:

> Explain how important fashion is to you
> How important is fashion to you? Choose one option:
  Important, No opinion, Not important.

The first question is an *open* question. This means that people can answer in any way they like. They could give a long answer. The second question is a *closed* question. This means that people must choose one of the answers provided.

You must check that your questions are clearly worded and that the person filling in the questionnaire knows exactly what is expected. Consider these questions:

> How much do you spend on clothes?
> How much do you spend on clothes each month?

The second question is clearer and will give more useful results.
  You also need to be careful not to ask leading questions:

> Gucci are the best designer. Do you agree?
> Who is your favourite designer?

The first question is leading the person to answer in a certain way. The second question is a much better way of asking the question.

Designing the layout

The final stage is to decide how you want the questionnaires to look on the page. It is a good idea to plan the design first. You should:

> put the questions in a logical order
> allow enough space for people to put in their answers
> put a title on so people know what it is about
> give clear instructions about how to fill it in.

Once you have designed the questionnaire, you can create it using any software that you think is suitable.

 Practical Task: Changing a questionnaire

In this task you will be asked to suggest improvements that could be made to a questionnaire. Open the 'Changing a questionnaire' worksheet on the website and follow the instructions.

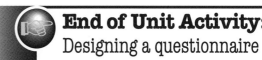 **End of Unit Activity:** Designing a questionnaire

In this activity you will be asked to design a questionnaire to find out what young people think about fashion. Open the 'Designing a questionnaire' worksheet on the website and follow the instructions.

4.2 Creating a data structure

In this unit you will learn how to:
> **Structure the data that you collect**
> **Decide who to ask**

Data structures

In Unit 4.1, we looked at how to ask questions. When the answers are stored on a computer, the data have to be set up (structured) in a certain way. For example, if we ask someone for their age on a questionnaire, we could ask them:

How old are you?	☐☐ years
How old are you?	☐ 0–18 ☐ 36–55
	☐ 19–35 ☐ 56 and over

The way that the answers are stored is known as a 'data type'. The first option asks the person for a number. This is known as a number (or numeric) type. The second option asks the person to tick the appropriate box. This is a multiple-choice data type.
  There are five main data types to choose from:

> **Text** – people can answer using letters and numbers
> **Number (Numeric)** – people can only answer with a number
> **Yes/No** – people must answer yes or no
> **Multiple Choice** – people are given options to choose from. You can let them tick one option or several options
> **Date** – people must answer with a date format, e.g. dd/mm/yyyy.

Choosing the data type

When you set up your questionnaire, you should choose the correct type for people to fill in. Sometimes this is very obvious. For example:

> If you are asking someone his or her name, you would use a **text** data type
> If you are asking someone if they like chips, a **Yes/No** data type is most suitable.

Sometimes it is not so obvious. For example, when asking for their age, do you choose number or multiple choice?

You should make it as easy as possible for people to fill in your questionnaire. For example, using a multiple-choice question may be easier than having to write lots of text.

You also need to think about how easy it will be to look through all the results later on. For example, if you ask the question: 'What do you think about global warming?', some people might write a lot of text and it might be difficult to understand. It might be better to do it as a multiple choice question.

Sampling

You cannot give your questionnaire to everyone, so you need to choose a sample of people to give it to. Look at the two results below, which are from a questionnaire about homework:

> 50% of people think that Year 11 do more homework than Year 7.
> Sample: 10 pupils in Year 7.
> 80% of people think that Year 11 do more homework than Year 7.
> Sample: 50 pupils in Year 7 and 50 pupils in Year 11.

Which result do you think is the most reliable?

It is important that you ask the right people, and that your sample size (the number of people you ask) is big enough for you to be confident about the results. In this case, the second result is more reliable as it used a sample of Year 7 and Year 11 pupils and quite a large number were asked.

Written Task: Data types and sampling

In this task you will be asked to decide what data types to use when collecting data and work out who you should ask to fill in your questionnaire. Open the 'Data types and sampling' worksheet on the website and follow the instructions.

End of Unit Activity: Setting up a data structure

In this activity you will be asked to design and create a questionnaire and data structure from scratch. Open the 'Setting up a data structure' worksheet on the website and follow the instructions.

4.3 | Entering and checking data

Learning Objectives

In this unit you will learn how to:
> **Check that data are correct**
> **Check that data are plausible**
> **Prevent errors in data**
> **Set up validation checks in Excel**

Entering data

After a questionnaire has been created, it is filled in by lots of people. When we have collected all of their answers, we can type them into the computer where they are stored as 'data'. A collection of data is called a 'database'.

It is very important that the data that we collect are typed in correctly. For example, let's say that John Smith filled in a questionnaire about school transport. Here are the answers he gave:

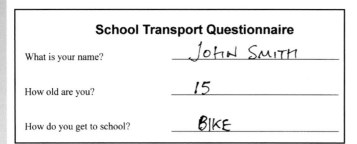

School Transport Questionnaire

What is your name? _John Smith_

How old are you? _15_

How do you get to school? _BIKE_

Figure 1 How does John get to school?

	A	C	E
1	**Name**	**Age**	**How they travel to school**
2	John Smith	150	Byke
3	Ralph Hope	15	Car
4	Amy Sole	16	Walk
5	Nita Ramprakash	15	Bike
6	Lucy Chan	16	Bus

Figure 2 Spot the errors

Someone has typed his answers into a database using Microsoft Excel. Can you spot any errors?
A database could have all sorts of errors in it. Some of these might be because the database was not set up properly in the first place; others because whoever typed in the answers, typed them in incorrectly.

If the data are wrong, it could lead to problems when the database is used. For example, if there was an error on a medical database, it could be very dangerous.

Written Task: Database errors

In this task you will be asked to spot errors that have been made in a database. Open the 'Database errors' worksheet on the website and follow the instructions.

Checking for errors

You should always check a database for errors before you start using it. You should do this whether you make the database yourself or whether you are using someone else's database. If there are errors in the data, then you will get the wrong results when you are looking at the data.

In Figure 2, you can see that 'Byke' is spelt incorrectly. If you search the database to find out how many people use a 'Bike' to get to school, it will not count John Smith and the results will be wrong.

The age data is also wrong. According to the database, John Smith is 150 years old. This is implausible, which means that it is not possible for it to be correct. If you search the database to find out the oldest person who answered the questionnaire, it would say that it was John Smith. In fact, he is only 15 years old.

Preventing errors

It is possible to prevent some errors from happening in the first place. You can add validation checks to the database. This means that the computer will check the data as it is typed in and tell you if there are any errors.

	A	C	E	F
1	Name	Age	How they travel to school	
2	John Smith	150	Bike	
3	Ralph Hope	15	Bike	
4	Amy Sole	16	Walk	
5	Nita Ramprakash	15	Car / Bike	
6	Lucy Chan	16	Walk	
7				

Figure 3 A drop-down list ensures the data are valid

For example, with the 'Byke' example, if the database has been set up with a drop-down list, it would be impossible for someone to type in the wrong answer, as they must choose an option from the list.

With the age, the database could have a *range check*, which means that it will only let you type in numbers within a certain range. In this example, the questionnaire is designed for school pupils, so the range could be set between 11 and 18 years of age. Range checks can also be used if the answer is a date or a time.

 **Skills Tutorial 1** This tutorial shows you how to add validation checks to a database in Excel.

 End of Unit Activity: Validation checks

In this activity you will be asked to check that data are correct and plausible. You will also be asked to set up validation checks. Open the 'Validation checks' worksheet on the website and follow the instructions.

4.4 Sorting and searching a database

Learning Objectives	In this unit you will learn how to:
	> **Sort a database**
	> **Search a database**
	> **Use the 'sort' and 'filter' options in Excel**

Examining a database

A database or dataset is a collection of data on a related topic. For example:

> A school database stores details about pupils
> A doctor's database stores details about patients and their medical conditions
> You have been using databases in this module to store the results from questionnaires.

The reason for having any database is so that it can be sorted or searched to find information from it. For example:

> The school might want to search the database to find everyone who is in Year 7
> Your doctor might sort the medical database to find out when you last had a tetanus injection
> You could search the results from the school transport survey to find out how many people come to school by bus.

Figure 1 A database is made up of fields and records

Microsoft Excel - Book1

File Edit View Insert Format Tools Data FlashPaper Window Help

K24

	A	B	C	D	E	F	G
1	**First Name**	**Last Name**	**Age**	**Gender**	**Favourite sport**	**Hours played a week**	**Club member**
2	Mohammed	Ali	15	M	Netball	2	Y
3	Letsenyane	Badule	13	F	Basketball	4	Y
4	Belinda	Bling	17	F	Netball	3	N
5	Bryony	Bridlington	13	F	Hockey	5	Y
6	Reg	Burton	15	M	Cricket	4	Y
7	Ruth	Burton	15	F	Football	3	Y
8	Lucy	Chan	13	F	Hockey	2	N
9	Luke	Chatterton	13	M	Football	3	N

Databases are made up of fields and records:

> A field is one item of information, e.g. first name, age, etc.
> A record is all of the information for one person.

If the database is in Excel, the columns are the fields and the rows are the records. The database opposite shows the results of a sports questionnaire that was filled in by around 120 school pupils.

Sorting

Sorting is when the data are ordered on one field. At the moment the data are sorted in alphabetical order using 'Last Name'. If you look at the last names, they start at A, then B, and so on.

You could sort the data on the 'Age' field so that the data are in age order. You can sort in ascending order (lowest first) or descending order (highest first). For example, if you sorted it in ascending order on the 'Age' field, the database would be sorted from youngest to oldest.

Skills Tutorial 1

This tutorial shows you how to sort data using Excel.

Searching

Searching is when you look through the database for particular information. For example, if we wanted to know how many people are female, we could search the 'Gender' field for everyone who has put 'F' for female. You can search on any field. Other examples for searches we could do using this database are:

> How many people are members of a club?
> How many people play five or more hours of sport a week?

You can search for more than one thing at a time. For example:

> How many people are female AND like football?
> How many people like netball OR hockey?

Skills Tutorial 2

This tutorial shows you how to search a database using Excel.

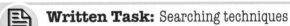

Written Task: Searching techniques

In this task you will be asked to carry out some searches. Open the 'Searching techniques' worksheet on the website and follow the instructions.

End of Unit Activity:

Searching and sorting

In this activity you will be asked to search and sort a database to find the answers to questions. Open the 'Searching and sorting' worksheet on the website and follow the instructions.

4.5

Creating new information from data

In this unit you will learn how to:
> **Create extra information from data**
> **Calculate averages**
> **Look at trends in data**

Introduction to calculations

It is possible to do calculations using the data in a database to create new information. For example, in the Sports Survey Results database, we can find out the oldest and youngest person by doing a search or a sort. It might be useful to know the average age as well. This information does not exist yet, so we would need to do a calculation to find it out.

Calculating averages

It is possible to work out the average for any of the questions that have a number as the answer. On the Sports Survey Results database we could work out:

> the average age of people who answered the questionnaire
> the average amount of time spent playing a sport.

The average age is worked out by adding up all of the ages and then dividing by the number of people. This can be done in Excel, as shown in Figure 1.

Figure 1 Calculating the average age

119	Nimra	Tan	17	F	Netball	2	N
120	Laura	Taylor	14	F	Netball	3	Y
121	Jey	Thomspon	15	M	Basketball	2	Y
122	Ryan	Todd	18	M	Hockey	3	Y
123	Heather	Tucker	15	F	Basketball	3	N
124	Heather	Tucker	16	F	Football	2	N
125	Zoe	Tung	12	F	Netball	2	N
126	Tina	Unsworth	18	F	Hockey	4	N
127	Jennifer	Wakefield	14	F	Other	2	Y
128	Stephen	Willingham	14	M	Football	2	Y
129	Tina	Wong	16	F	Netball	3	Y
130			=average(C2:C129)				
131							

Skills Tutorial 1

This tutorial shows you how to calculate an average using Excel.

In this case, the average age of the people who filled in the questionnaire is 14.65 years old. This means that this database is quite good at telling us about younger people's sport activities, but you couldn't really use it to work out the kind of sports that older people are playing.

	A	B	C	D	E	
1	**Holiday destinations**	**2004**	**2005**	**2006**	**2007**	
2	Number of people who went to America	45	48	47	43	
3	Number of people who went to Australia	55	72	88	100	
4	Number of people who went to Europe	67	64	65	67	
5	Number of people who went to Asia	32	57	89	120	
6	Number of people who stayed in UK	87	76	65	43	

Figure 2 Holiday company database

Written Task:
Predicting a trend

In this task you will be asked to predict a trend by looking at some information in a database. Open the 'Predicting a trend' worksheet on the website and follow the instructions.

Working out a trend

A trend is the general direction in which things are going. You might have heard the word when people talk about fashion. A trend in fashion is the type of clothes people are wearing these days.

We can use data to *predict* trends. This means that we are making an estimate of what might happen in the future. Look at the example above. It is from a database used by a travel agency. They use it to predict where their customers will be going on holiday. Look at the number of people who went to Asia in 2004. Then look at how this number goes up each year. Can you see the trend? What do you think will happen in 2008?

It is sometimes useful to create graphs when trying to predict a trend. For example, we could plot the data for Asia on a line graph. This makes it easier to see the trend and to predict what might happen next year.

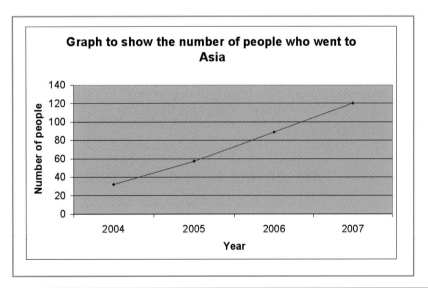

Figure 3 Graph of holiday predictions

End of Unit Activity: Predictions

In this activity you will be asked to make predictions based on information in a database. Open the 'Predictions' worksheet on the website and follow the instructions.

4.6

Reaching conclusions from data

In this unit you will learn how to:
> **Reach a conclusion from data**
> **Present conclusions**
> **Check that results are plausible**
> **Improve your data**

Reaching conclusions

A conclusion is when you come up with an answer to a question or hypothesis. Using the Sport Survey Results database we could test the hypothesis: 'More boys than girls like football'. You would need to carry out some searches on the database first and then you could reach a conclusion. In this case, the conclusion is either that the hypothesis is *true* or that it is *false*.

The difficult bit is working out what searches you need to do to reach a conclusion. With the football hypothesis, we need to:

> do a search to count all the boys who like football
> do a search to count all the girls who like football
> see which search has the biggest number.

 Written Task: Reaching conclusions

In this task you will be asked to make a prediction and then test it using a database. Open the 'Reaching conclusions' worksheet on the website and follow the instructions.

If we did that we would find that there were 29 boys who said football was their favourite sport, compared to 11 girls. In this case, we can reach the conclusion that the hypothesis is *true*.

Presenting your conclusions

Once we have come to our conclusion, we need to present the results. You might do this by writing a report or producing a slideshow presentation. You should provide evidence that backs up your conclusion. It would not be enough to say that the hypothesis is true, you need to show the data that prove this, for example by using a table like the one shown here:

This tutorial shows you how to add and use tables in Word.

Number of girls whose favourite sport is football	11
Number of boys whose favourite sport is football	29
Total whose favourite sport is football	40

Source: Sport Survey Results.xls

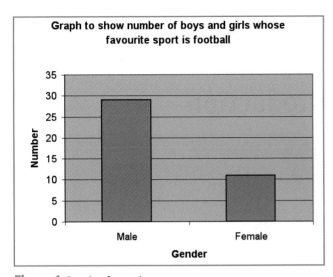

Figure 1 Graph of people whose favourite sport is football
Source: Sport Survey Results.xls

You could also produce a chart to present the results, like the one in Figure 1.

Checking that results are plausible

If something is plausible it means that it is believable. You should always look at the results and ask yourself whether they are plausible. In this case, we have found that more boys than girls like football. This seems to be plausible. If it were the other way round, would you still believe it?

For results to be plausible, you need to think about:

> Who was asked?
>> Did we ask enough people?
>> Was there an equal mix of boys and girls?

> Are there any errors in the data?
>> Could someone have made a mistake when they were typing in the data?
>> Does the database have validation checks on it?

Review and amend

You might find that you don't have all the data that you need to be able to make a conclusion. For example, in the Sports Survey:

> How popular is rugby? We don't know, because rugby wasn't one of the choices
> Do young people play similar sports to older people? We don't know, because we didn't ask any older people to fill in the questionnaire.

If you can't find the information you need, you might have to change the questions on the questionnaire and ask more people to fill it in for you. You can then do the searches, sorts and graphs again to try to find your conclusion.

End of Unit Activity: Presenting a conclusion

In this activity you will be asked to use a database to test a hypothesis and then present your results. Open the 'Presenting a conclusion' worksheet on the website and follow the instructions.

End of Module Assignment: Film database

In this assignment you will be asked to use a database of films to test a hypothesis and present your conclusions. Open the 'Module 4 assignment' worksheet on the website and follow the instructions.

5 CONTROL

Case Study introduction

This is Mike. He gets up at 7.30 a.m. every morning. We are going to fast-forward through a typical day for Mike. As we go, see if you can keep count of all the things that Mike comes across that are controlled by computers.

Mike gets up and has his breakfast. He loves porridge and he can do it in two minutes in his microwave. He jumps in his car.

Mike loves gadgets and his wife bought him a satellite navigation system last Christmas. It tells him to avoid the A15 as there is a traffic jam. He needs petrol, so he stops off at the local petrol station to fill up. He pays using his credit card. He hates having to remember all the numbers.

Figure 3 Car park barrier

He gets to work and pulls up to the car park barrier. It opens and he drives in to the car park. He reverses into a parking space. His car has parking sensors, which beep when he gets close to the wall. Mike is the manager of a factory that makes cars. The factory uses expensive robots that can put the cars together.

It's been a busy day for Mike, but now it's time to go home. On his way home, Mike stops in at the supermarket.

> **Q** How many different things did you count? What were they? In what ways might computers be used to control different things in the supermarket?

Mike walks up to the doors and they open for him automatically. After he has walked through they stay open for a few seconds and then close again. They keep doing this all day long. He grabs some food out of the freezer. The freezers are kept at a constant temperature all day and all night to keep the food frozen. He goes up to pay. He puts his food on the conveyer belt and it moves up to the cashier and stops. Mike pays using his card and sets off home.

Figure 4 Freezer compartment in the supermarket

> **Q** Why is it useful to use computers rather than people to control things? What problems might there be if any of the computer systems fail in the supermarket?

Mike has realised that all the devices work in a similar way. They all need some way of being switched on and told what to do. So his microwave and his alarm clock have buttons on them that the person can press. In fact, quite a lot of devices use buttons or keypads of some sort as a way of *inputting* instructions. After that, the device makes *decisions* about what it should do next: his microwave works out when two minutes have passed; his alarm clock works out when it is 7.30 a.m. Finally, all of the devices physically do something. They have an *output* of some description. So, the microwave cooks the food and then beeps when it has finished; the alarm clock sounds an alarm at 7.30 a.m.

Figure 5 Mike's microwave

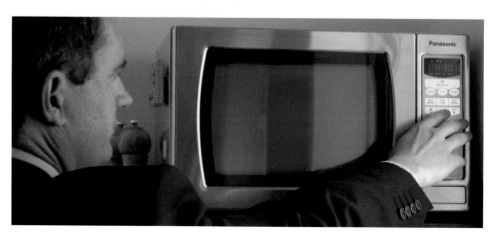

Q Describe the inputs and outputs for the other devices that we have talked about so far. How do the supermarket doors and car park barriers know when to open? Identify other control systems that work automatically in this way.

Figure 6 Factory robots can fit windscreens

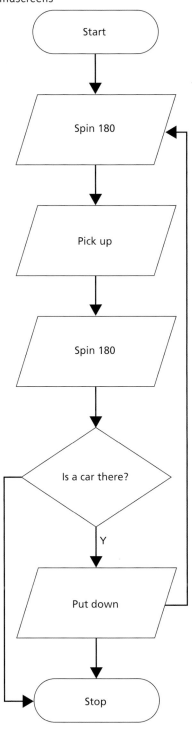

Mike is in charge of the production line at the car factory. He is in charge of programming the robots, that is, giving them instructions. The robots can spin around and they can pick up and put down objects.

He writes a program that gets the robot to pick up a windscreen and put it in the car. The instructions are:
SPIN 180, PICK UP, SPIN 180, PUT DOWN.

If this works, the robot will spin around and pick up a windscreen, spin back round again and place it in the car.

Q What would happen if the instructions were wrong? These instructions assume that the car is in the right place. What would happen if the car were not there? How could they stop this happening?

The instructions to control the robots are written using a flowchart. The flowchart in Figure 5 shows the instructions used to put the windscreens in the cars.

Figure 7 Flowchart for factory robot instructions

5.1 | Introduction to control and flowcharts

In this unit you will learn:
> How computers are used to control other devices
> How inputs, processes and outputs are used
> How to understand a flowchart
> How to amend a set of instructions in a flowchart

Introduction to computer control

Computers are used to control everything from DVD recorders to space shuttles. Computers control things by following instructions *programmed* in by a human being. For example, you can *program* a DVD recorder to record a certain channel at a certain time. Programming a space shuttle is a bit more tricky!

A *control system* is anything that is controlled by a computer. It is based on inputs, processes and outputs.

Figure 1 Parts of a control system

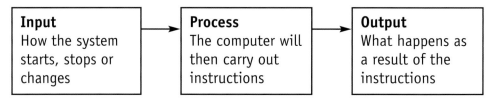

| **Input**
How the system starts, stops or changes | **Process**
The computer will then carry out instructions | **Output**
What happens as a result of the instructions |

For example, on most trains you have to press a button to open the doors:

> Input: the button is pressed
> Process: the computer sends an instruction to a motor, which controls the doors
> Output: the doors open.

Flowcharts

The instructions that the computer follows could just be written in a list like this:

1 If someone presses the 'Open' button then the doors should open.
2 The doors should stay open for a few seconds and then close again.
3 If no one presses any buttons, then the doors should stay closed.

A good way to show this is using a flowchart. Figure 2 shows a flowchart for the train doors.

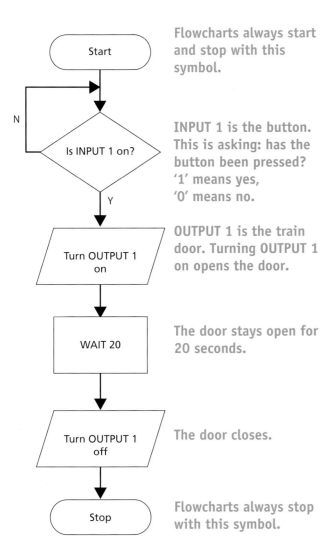

Flowcharts always start and stop with this symbol.

INPUT 1 is the button. This is asking: has the button been pressed? '1' means yes, '0' means no.

OUTPUT 1 is the train door. Turning OUTPUT 1 on opens the door.

The door stays open for 20 seconds.

The door closes.

Flowcharts always stop with this symbol.

Figure 2 Flowchart for the train doors

The symbols have different shapes as they mean different things (see Figure 3). The arrows show what step comes next. The decision box is the only one that can have two arrows coming out of it.

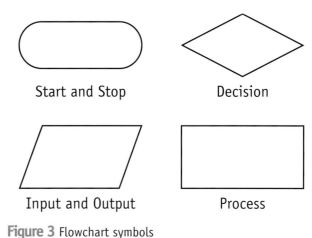

Figure 3 Flowchart symbols

You can create flowcharts using different types of software. Some software, such as Flowol or Logicator, are designed for flowcharting. The examples you have seen so far were created using Word.

 Skills Tutorial 1 This tutorial shows you how to create flowcharts in Word.

 **Written Task:** Changing the flowchart

In this task you will be asked to make changes to a flowchart. Open the 'Changing the flowchart' worksheet on the website and follow the instructions.

 End of Unit Activity: Adding a sensor

In this activity you will be asked to change a flowchart to include a sensor. Open the 'Adding a sensor' worksheet on the website and follow the instructions.

5.2 | Creating a flowchart

In this unit you will learn how to:
> **Design and create a flowchart**
> **Work with flowchart symbols**
> **Work with inputs and outputs**

Designing your own flowcharts

In this unit, you will design and make a flowchart from scratch. Flowcharts can be quite tricky to develop, so it is important that you design them on paper first. A good way to start is to write out what needs to happen as a list of instructions first, and then try to turn it into a flowchart.

For example, if you were designing a control system for a car park barrier, the steps might be:

 Written Task: Writing instructions

In this task you will be asked to write instructions for a computer-controlled system. Open the 'Writing instructions' worksheet on the website and follow the instructions.

1 The driver presses the button on the machine.
2 A ticket comes out of the slot on the machine.
3 The barrier opens.
4 The barrier stays open for 30 seconds.
5 The barrier closes.

Flowchart symbols

The next stage is to work out which symbol to use for each step.

Start and Stop: You need to put one of these at the beginning and at the end of every flowchart you create.

Input and Output: You would use one of these to show the button being pressed, one for the printer that prints the ticket and one for the barrier opening.

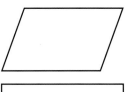

Process: You would use one of these to show the barrier staying open for 30 seconds.

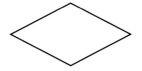

Decision: You would use one of these to show whether the button has been pressed or not.

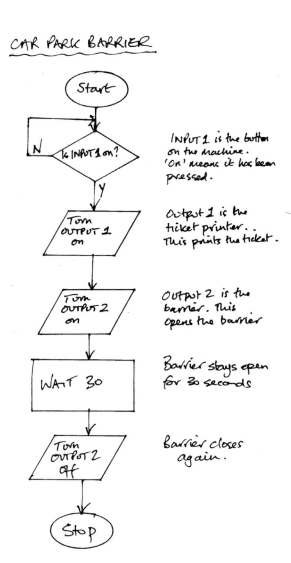

Figure 1 Sketch of a flowchart

Inputs and outputs

An input is needed to make a control system work. For example, the driver pressing the button on the machine is an input. If the driver did not press the button, the system would never start.

The output is what physically happens as a result of the input. In this case, after the button is pressed, a ticket is printed and the car park barrier opens.

So in this system we have:

> the button: which we call INPUT 1
> the printer: which we call OUTPUT1
> the barrier: which we call OUTPUT 2.

In the flowchart you have to state whether you want to turn the inputs on or off.

> 'Turn INPUT 1 on' means that the button has been pressed
> 'Turn OUTPUT 1 on' means that a ticket is printed out
> 'Turn OUTPUT 2 off' means that the barrier is closed.

Drawing a rough design

A rough design for the flowchart is shown in Figure 1.

> The correct symbol has been used for each step.
> The inputs and outputs have been given names.
> Comments have been added to make it clearer what happens at each step. This is called *annotation*.

Once your design is complete, you can start to create it using any software that you have available.

End of Unit Activity: Creating a flowchart

In this activity you will be asked to design a flowchart for a ticketing system. Open the 'Creating a flowchart' worksheet on the website and follow the instructions.

5.3

Using instructions that repeat

Learning Objectives

In this unit you will learn how to:
> **Create loops**
> **Create subroutines**

Loops

In ICT, if something is in a loop it means that when it gets to the end of the instructions, it will start all over again. Think about the car-park barrier that we looked at earlier; Figure 1 shows how it works.

Figure 1 The car-park barrier instructions repeat forever

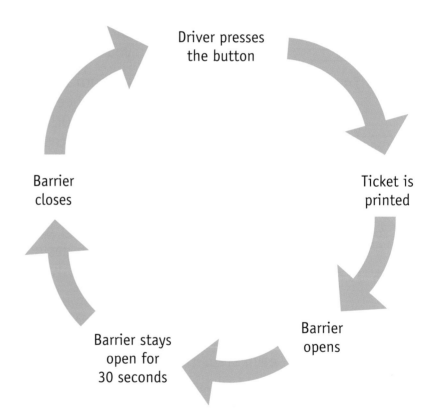

After the barrier has closed, the loop starts again when the next driver presses the button. It will go on like this forever, or until the whole system is switched off.

In a flowchart, you show loops using arrows. To create a loop for the car park barrier machine, an arrow is added (see Figure 2).

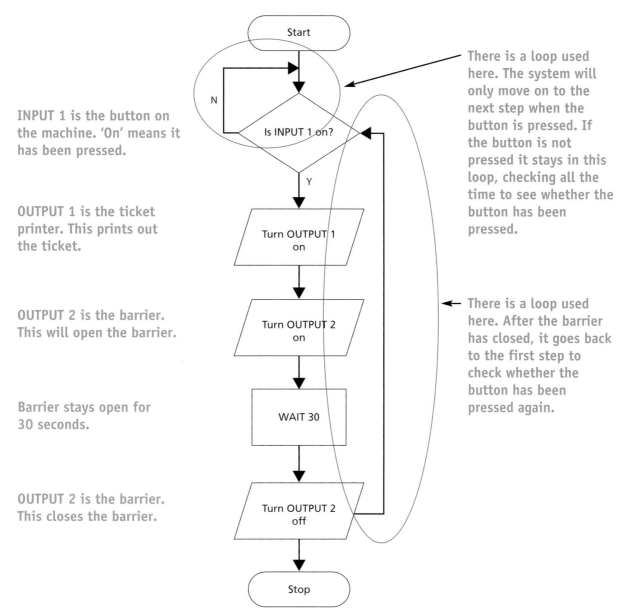

INPUT 1 is the button on the machine. 'On' means it has been pressed.

OUTPUT 1 is the ticket printer. This prints out the ticket.

OUTPUT 2 is the barrier. This will open the barrier.

Barrier stays open for 30 seconds.

OUTPUT 2 is the barrier. This closes the barrier.

There is a loop used here. The system will only move on to the next step when the button is pressed. If the button is not pressed it stays in this loop, checking all the time to see whether the button has been pressed.

There is a loop used here. After the barrier has closed, it goes back to the first step to check whether the button has been pressed again.

Figure 2 Flowchart for the looping car-park barrier instructions

Subroutines

There will be times when you are creating flowcharts, when you find that you are repeating the same steps over and over again. If this happens, you should use a subroutine to make your flowchart more efficient.

For example, the flowchart in Figure 3 is for a burglar alarm for a house. There is an infrared beam on the front door and on the back door. If either beam detects movement, the alarm sounds until someone switches it off. The steps to make the alarm sound are the same for the front door and the back door, so instead of writing them out twice, you put them in a subroutine.

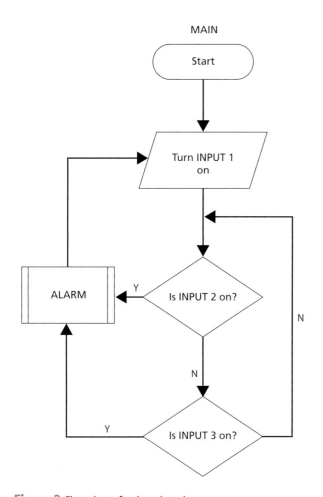

INPUT 1 is the on/off switch for the burglar alarm. This switches it on.

INPUT 2 is the infrared sensor on the front door. This checks whether it has detected movement. It if has, then the ALARM subroutine runs. If not, it goes on to the next step.

INPUT 3 is the infrared sensor on the back door. This checks whether it has detected movement. It if has, then the ALARM subroutine runs. If not, it loops back and checks INPUT 2 again.

Figure 3 Flowchart for burglar alarm

Figure 4 A car park barrier

ALARM SUBROUTINE

```
            ( Start )
                │
                ▼
        ┌───────────────┐
        │ Turn OUTPUT 1 │          OUTPUT 1 is the alarm.
     ┌─▶│     on        │          This means that it will sound.
     │  └───────────────┘
     │          │
     │          ▼
     │       ◇─────────◇           INPUT 1 is the on/off switch. This
   N │      ╱           ╲          checks whether it has been swithced
     └─────◇ Is INPUT 1 off? ◇     off. It if has, the alarm will stop
            ╲           ╱          sounding. If not, it carries on.
             ◇─────────◇
                │ Y
                ▼                   The alarm is switched off. You now
        ┌───────────────┐          go back to the MAIN flowchart and
        │ Turn OUTPUT 1 │          follow the arrow. This takes you
        │     off        │         back to the start.
        └───────────────┘
                │
                ▼
            ( Stop )
```

Figure 5 Flowchart for alarm subroutine

Written Task: Subroutines
In this task you will be asked to create a flowchart with a subroutine. Open the 'Subroutines' worksheet on the website and follow the instructions.

End of Unit Activity: Repeating instructions
In this activity you will be asked to design a flowchart for a top-secret laboratory. You must include a loop and a subroutine. Open the 'Repeating instructions' worksheet on the website and follow the instructions.

5.4 Working with variables

In this unit you will learn:
> **What a variable is**
> **How variables can be used in flowcharts**
> **How variables can affect what happens in a flowchart**

What is a variable?

A variable is a piece of data that might change over time. For example, in a central heating system, we could have a variable called 'temperature'. The value of 'temperature' would be set by taking a reading from a sensor. The value would be changing all the time, depending on whether the heating was on or off. We could use this variable to decide what should happen. For example:

> Temperature = 18 degrees: turn Heating ON
> Temperature = 25 degrees: turn Heating OFF

Written Task: Working with variables

In this task you will be asked to create a flowchart using a variable. Open the 'Working with variables' worksheet on the website and follow the instructions.

In Figure 2, a variable is being used to count how many times a person types their PIN code into a cash machine. After three attempts, the cash machine keeps the card if the correct PIN has not been entered. The variable is called COUNTER because that's what it is doing – counting.

Figure 1 A central heating system with the wrong settings!

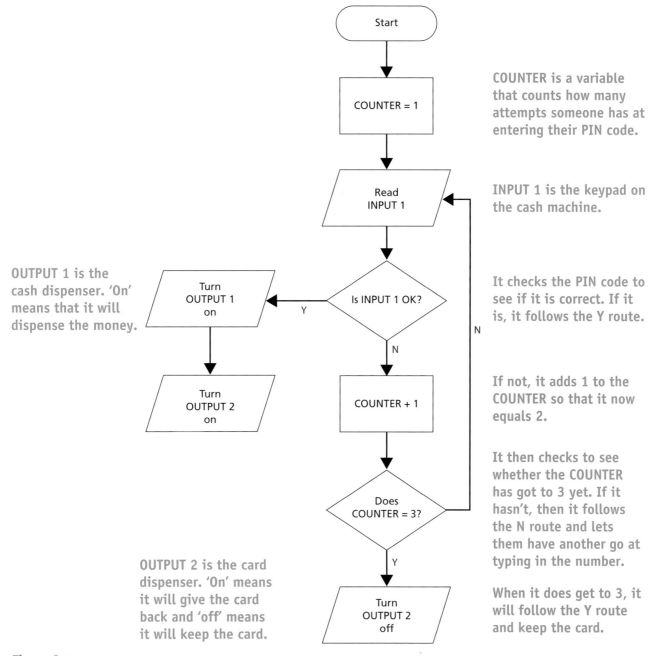

COUNTER is a variable that counts how many attempts someone has at entering their PIN code.

INPUT 1 is the keypad on the cash machine.

OUTPUT 1 is the cash dispenser. 'On' means that it will dispense the money.

It checks the PIN code to see if it is correct. If it is, it follows the Y route.

If not, it adds 1 to the COUNTER so that it now equals 2.

It then checks to see whether the COUNTER has got to 3 yet. If it hasn't, then it follows the N route and lets them have another go at typing in the number.

OUTPUT 2 is the card dispenser. 'On' means it will give the card back and 'off' means it will keep the card.

When it does get to 3, it will follow the Y route and keep the card.

Figure 2 Flowchart for cash machine

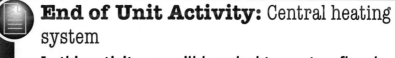

End of Unit Activity: Central heating system

In this activity you will be asked to create a flowchart that can be used to control a central heating system. Open the 'Central heating system' worksheet on the website and follow the instructions.

5.5 | Testing instructions and using feedback

Learning Objectives

In this unit you will learn:
> **How to test and refine instructions**
> **What a simulation is**
> **How to use feedback in a control system**

Testing instructions

You should test your flowcharts to make sure that they work properly. How you test them depends on what facilities and software you have in your school.

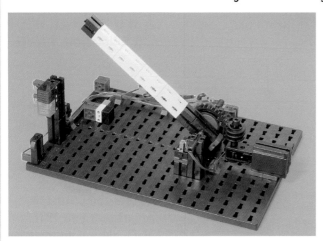

Figure 1 Car-park barrier model

You may have control equipment, similar to that shown in Figure 1, that you can connect to your computer. You can then run your flowchart and the model will move. You can then see for real whether it works or not.

You may have specialised software, such as Logicator or Flowol, that use *simulations* like the ones shown in Figure 2. This means that when the flowchart is run, it will show you what would happen in real life using graphics.

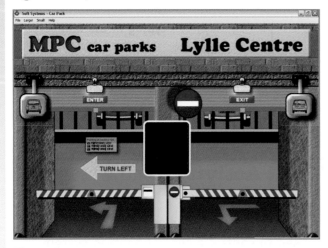
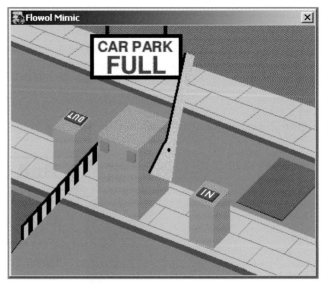

Figure 2 Simulations running in Logicator and Flowol

If you have these options then you can check your flowcharts yourself by following through each step. Another method is *peer review*. This means that you ask someone else in your class to check it for you, while you check theirs.

Whichever method you use, you should make any changes necessary to make sure that your flowchart works properly and efficiently. This means making use of *loops* and *subroutines* where possible.

Using feedback

Figure 3 iRobot Dirt Dog vacuum cleaner

In a control system, things change all the time. For example, the car park barrier goes up and down all the time. We need to know whether it is up or down. There is no point telling the barrier to go up if it is up already! If we tell the barrier to go down when there is a car underneath, it could be dangerous.

This is where feedback comes in. Feedback is when information is received from a sensor. The control system then decides what it should do. For example, Figure 3 is a picture of the iRobot Dirt Dog vacuum cleaner. It works like this:

> It moves around the room and vacuums the floor
> It receives *feedback* from sensors that tell it if there is an obstacle in the way or if it reaches a wall
> If it detects an obstacle or a wall it changes direction.

 Written Task: Controlling a robot

In this task you will be asked to create a flowchart to control a robotic vacuum cleaner. Open the 'Controlling a robot' worksheet on the website and follow the instructions.

 End of Unit Activity: Robot lawnmower

In this activity you will be asked to create a flowchart that can be used to control a robotic lawnmower. You must ask someone to test your flowchart. Open the 'Robot lawnmower' worksheet on the website and follow the instructions.

 End of Module Assignment: Air bags

In this assignment you will be asked to create a flowchart to control the air bags in a car. Open the 'Module 5 assignment' worksheet on the website and follow the instructions.

Case Study introduction

Figure 1 Vincent and Andy

This is Vincent and Andy. They have been friends since primary school. Like lots of people their age, they are into computers and technology. Vincent has got the latest games console and often plays games with people all over the world. The family also have a PC connected to the Internet.

> **Q** What kinds of things do you think Vincent might use his PC for? What other examples of computer technology do you think Vincent might have?

Vincent's mum is a dentist. She's just got back from work. She worries about how much time Vincent spends 'messing about on computers'. Vincent can't see the problem. After all, his mum uses computers quite a lot at work herself.

> **Q** In what ways might Vincent's mum use ICT at work? Identify all the different ways that you can communicate with other people over the Internet. In what ways might email be used for personal or work reasons?

Figure 2 Mum's email inbox

Vincent's mum goes to the computer and loads her email software. She looks in her inbox, which is full of messages. Some messages are from people she knows and some aren't.

> **Q** Why might Vincent's mum get emails from people she doesn't know? What might be the problems with these emails? What can she do about it?

Vincent and Andy decide to get on with their homework. They have been asked by their History teacher to find some information about Nazi Germany. Vincent and Andy do a bit of Internet searching to find what they need. They then copy and paste what they have found into a word-processed document.

> **Q** What problems might Vincent and Andy have if they are using the Internet to find information for this homework? What can they do about these problems?

When the homework is finished Vincent and Andy decide to spend some time on the Internet.

They do this quite a lot in the evenings, as lots of their school friends are online. They also have quite a few friends who they have met online. They meet most of them through online games websites and chat rooms. They sometimes find themselves chatting with people that they don't know.

> **Q** Why might Vincent and Andy be at risk when they are online? What can they do to keep themselves safe when they are online?

6.1 Uses of ICT in the wider world

Learning Objectives

In this unit you will learn:
> **How ICT can be used in the home**
> **How ICT can be used at work**
> **To compare the use of ICT inside and outside school**

Introduction to using ICT outside school

In this book, we have covered:

> Presenting information: using word-processing, desktop-publishing and presentation software
> Selecting and using information: from websites, databases and other sources
> Modelling: using spreadsheets
> Data handling: using spreadsheets
> Control: using flowcharts.

It is important to realise that ICT is being used by lots of different people and organisations all over the world. This unit looks at some of the many ways that ICT is used outside school.

ICT at home

You may use ICT quite a lot at home. For example, you may use the Internet to find information for homework and then use word-processing to present the information.

You may use ICT at home in a very different way to how you use it at school. For example, you may view videos, listen to music, talk with your friends or play games.

If you don't have a computer at home, you may use other computer-controlled devices, such as MP3 players, DVDs or microwaves.

Written Task: ICT at home

In this task you will be asked to think about the ways that you use ICT at home. Open the 'ICT at home' worksheet on the website and follow the instructions.

The things you do at home may seem very different, but they require the same skills and knowledge as the things you do at school.

For example:

> If you download music, you will have a list of all your tracks – this is a database
> If you play computer games – this is a computer model
> If you use a mobile phone or MP3 player – this is computer control.

ICT at work

ICT is critical for many people's work. There are hardly any jobs these days that do not involve the use of ICT. For example:

> Businesses use websites to sell things to customers
> The government uses spreadsheets for financial information
> Hospitals use databases for patient information
> The RAF uses sophisticated control systems for aeroplanes
> Publishers use desktop-publishing software to produce magazines and newspapers.

Many people use exactly the same software for work that you use at school. This means that learning ICT at school gives you the skills and knowledge to get all sorts of jobs.

How the police use ICT

The UK police force uses ICT in many different ways:

> They use databases to help fight crime. For example, the Police National Computer contains information about criminals
> They use websites to provide members of the public with useful information, for example, how to prevent crime
> They use computer control systems. For example, they use CCTV to monitor areas where there is a lot of crime and speed cameras on dangerous roads.

 Written Task: ICT at work

In this task you will be asked to think about the ways that ICT can be used at work. Open the 'ICT at work' worksheet on the website and follow the instructions.

Figure 1 Computers can help fight crime

 End of Unit Activity: Hospitals

In this activity you will be asked to think about all the ways in which a hospital could use ICT. Open the 'Hospitals' worksheet on the website and follow the instructions.

6.2 | Using email and other methods of communication

Learning Objectives

In this unit you will learn:

> **How we can use the Internet to communicate with other people**
> **How to use email to send and receive messages and attachments**
> **How email is used in the wider world**
> **What problems might happen when communicating**

Introduction

We can use the Internet to communicate with other people all over the world. We can send and receive text, video and sound messages. It is also possible to send and receive files over the Internet. For example, you could send a movie of your family to a relative who lives in a different country.

This unit looks at some of the ways that we can communicate, concentrating mainly on email. Before we go onto email it is worth thinking about the other methods of communication and what they are used for:

> **Chat rooms:** websites where you go into a virtual room to talk to other people.
> **Messenger services:** services that send instant messages between people who are online.
> **Social networks/blogs:** websites, such as MySpace and Bebo, where people can put information about themselves or a blog, which is like an online diary.
> **Newsgroups/forums:** websites where you can post and read . messages on different topics.
> **Video conferencing:** where people can see and speak to each other using webcams.

Email

Email is software that lets you send and receive messages and files to and from other people. Email has become an important way of communicating for individuals and for big organisations.

Many people use email to keep in touch with family and friends and to send and receive files. A file is anything that is stored on your computer, e.g. a spreadsheet file, a movie file or a sound file.

Figure 1 Email keeps us in touch, wherever we are in the world

Figure 1 Email keeps us in touch, wherever we are in the world

People who work in organisations also use email to help them in their work. For example, a manager might have a spreadsheet file that they want someone else to work on. The manager could email the instructions to the person, sending the spreadsheet file as an attachment. When the person receives the email, they read the message and then open the attachment. They can then save the file to their own computer.

Problems with email

Email is very popular, but there are some problems with it:

> Some people don't have email, which means you can't communicate with them
> Emails can contain *viruses*, which can harm your computer
> If the attachments are large files, e.g. video, they can take a long time to send
> Emails are not 100% secure. This means that someone could read your emails and, maybe, steal your personal information
> There is a lot of junk email, called *spam*.

Written Task:
Communications

In this task you will be asked to think about the ways in which you can use ICT to communicate. Open the 'Communications' worksheet on the website and follow the instructions.

End of Unit Activity: Bigg Computers

In this activity you will be asked to think about the ways in which a business can use ICT to communicate. Open the 'Bigg Computers' worksheet on the website and follow the instructions.

6.3

Staying safe online

In this unit you will learn:
> **What risks there are on the Internet**
> **How to stay safe on the Internet**
> **What you can do if you feel threatened**

Introduction to staying safe

Most people think that the Internet is a brilliant invention. We can use it for lots of good reasons, whether it is for schoolwork or just for fun. Unfortunately there are people out there who use the Internet for the wrong reasons and these people can put you or your computer at risk.

The risks include:

> your computer getting a virus
> someone using your personal details to steal money from you or your family
> someone finding out who you are and where you live because they want to harm you.

This unit gets you to think about some of the risks that exist and how you can protect yourself so that they do not happen to you.

Practical Task: The risk test

In this task you can work out whether you are at risk when you are using the Internet. Open the 'The risk test' worksheet on the website and follow the instructions.

Figure 1 You are also at risk when using your mobile phone

When am I at risk?

Every time you are online (connected to the Internet) you are at risk. It doesn't really matter what you are doing – perhaps you are viewing a website, chatting on MSN, downloading some music, or writing your blog. If you are online – you are at risk.

You are also at risk when you are using your mobile phone for calls or texts.

Personal information

Never give out your personal information online. Personal information is anything that would identify you (or your friends). This includes:

> Your real name
> Your address
> Which school you go to
> Photographs of yourself or your friends
> Your age
> Any financial information (yours or your parents')
> Personal thoughts.

Do you know who you are talking to?

It is easy to meet people online. Perhaps you met them in a chat room, on MSN or through an online game. They might be the same age as you and seem nice. They might also be lying. They might be saying all the right things to win your trust.

Remember that you never really know who you are talking to when you are online. So:

> **Never** arrange to meet someone that you have met online
> **Never** give out any personal information.

Cyberbullying

Cyberbullying is when a bully uses some form of technology to carry out the bullying. Cyberbullies use email, texts, chat rooms, messaging software or even weblogs to say hurtful things about other people.

If this happens to you then you should speak to a teacher, parent, adult or older pupil that you trust. There are people who will support you and can stop the bullying.

You should show respect to everyone else whether they are online or not – and you should get that respect back.

 Written Task: Where to get help
In this task you can work out where to get help if you feel that you are at risk when using the Internet. Open the 'Where to get help' worksheet on the website and follow the instructions.

Undesirable content

Lots of websites are not suitable for school or home. Sometimes you come across them by accident. These websites have violent or pornographic images. Some of these websites are illegal.

Some people who have extreme views, like racist groups, use the Internet to spread their ideas. Sometimes they trick you into reading their sites. For example, the website might look like it is about football but when you start reading it you realise that it is racist. Remember the work you did in Unit 2.3 on finding out who is behind a website.

If you come across any of these sites, close your browser or switch off your screen and report it to a teacher.

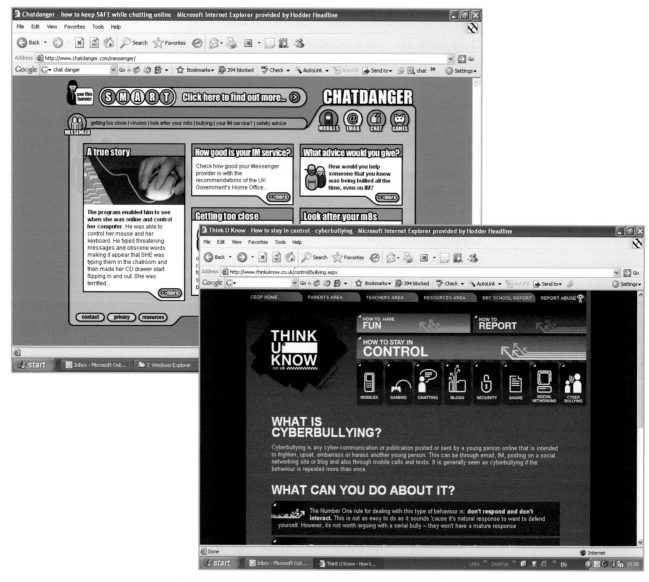

Figure 2 There are websites that give information about staying safe online, such as www.chatdanger.com, set up by ChildNet International, and www.thinkuknow.co.uk, set up by the Child Exploitation and Online Protection Centre

Threats to your computer

Your computer is also at risk, from viruses and other similar problems. A virus is a program that installs itself on your computer without you knowing it. It can destroy everything on your computer. Many viruses come from emails, gaming sites and download sites. Many download sites are illegal and are very likely to contain viruses.

To avoid viruses, you can use anti-virus software. You should only download from legal sites, which are usually the ones that you have to pay for.

Figure 2 Your computer is also at risk

 End of Unit Activity: Internet use at school

In this activity you will be asked to think about what you are and are not allowed to do using the school computers. Open the 'Internet use at school' worksheet on the website and follow the instructions.

 End of Module Assignment: ICT in the wider world

In this assignment you will be asked to think about the ways in which computers are used in school, at home and at work. You will also be asked to consider situations where it would be better not to use a computer. Open the 'Module 6 assignment' worksheet on the website and follow the instructions.

KEYWORDS GLOSSARY

Unit	Keyword	Definition
1.1	Audience	The people that will be looking at what you have made using ICT
1.1	Images	Pictures
1.1	Presentation	A slideshow of information
1.1	Purpose	The reason that something is being done, e.g. a presentation
1.1	Slides	Pages used in a slideshow
1.1	Slideshow	A number of pages of information
1.1	Style	The manner of design
1.1	Text	Writing that appears on the screen or in print
1.2	Animations	The way in which text and images appear in a slideshow
1.2	Background colour	The colour of the slide or page
1.2	ClipArt	A library of images
1.2	Font colour	The colour of the text
1.2	Font size	The size of the text
1.2	Font style	The style of the text
1.2	Multimedia	The presentation of information using text, graphics, animations and video
1.2	Template	A layout that you can use for slides in a slideshow
1.2	Title slide	The first page of a slideshow
1.2	Transition	The way that the slides change in a slideshow
1.2	WordArt	A way of creating special effects with text
1.3	Consistency	Making sure that all slides are similar in terms of their layout
1.3	Slide master	The main slide used to set the format of all slides in a slideshow
1.4	Content	The information that appears on a slide
1.4	Copyright	The right of the person who owns the information
1.4	Cropping	Cutting parts off an image
1.4	Impact	To have a strong effect
1.4	Re-sizing	Making an image bigger or smaller
1.4	Summarise	To reduce the amount of information without losing the meaning
1.5	Adapt	Change
2.1	Address	A way of finding a webpage on the Internet
2.1	Favourites	A way of creating links to webpages if you want to go back to them again
2.1	Hits	The number of websites that might be relevant after a search has been done
2.1	Internet	A global connection of computers
2.1	Keywords	Words used to search with when using the Internet
2.1	Refine	Make changes that improve something
2.1	Relevance	How suitable information is
2.1	Reliability	Whether you can trust information to be true
2.1	Search engine	A way of finding information on the Internet by typing in keywords
2.1	Sources of information	Places where you can get information from
2.2	Advanced search	A way of carrying out a more complicated search
2.2	Image search	A way of searching the Internet just for pictures

2.2	Speech marks	Put them around words in a search engine to make the search more specific
2.2	The + sign	Use it in a search engine to make sure words are included
2.2	The – sign	Use it in a search engine to make sure words are NOT included
2.2	Thumbnail	A small image that you can click on so that you can see a larger image
2.3	Accurate	Correct
2.3	Bias	Where information is given from one point of view
2.4	Frames	Boxes used to put information and images in using DTP
2.4	Plan	A method of working out how to do something before you start
2.5	Column	In DTP – a vertical line of text on a page
2.6	Layering	Text or images that overlap each other
2.5	Leaflet	A type of publication – a small printed sheet
2.6	Overlap	Text or images that are on top of each other
2.5	Picture frame	In DTP – a box for putting pictures in
2.5	Poster	A type of publication – usually pinned up on a wall
2.6	Rotate	Turn image or text
2.5	Table frame	In DTP – a box for putting a table of information in
2.5	Text flow	Text that automatically moves from one text frame to another
2.5	Text frame	In DTP – a box for putting text in
2.5	WordArt frame	In DTP – a box for creating special effects with text
2.6	Wrap	The way that text is positioned around other text or images
3.1	Cell	One box in a spreadsheet where a column and row meet
3.1	Cell reference	The way of identifying a cell, e.g. A1
3.1	Column	A vertical line of numbers or text
3.1	Formula	A calculation
3.1	Formulae	The plural of formula - calculations
3.1	Row	A horizontal line of numbers or text
3.1	Spreadsheet	Software used mainly to deal with numbers
3.1	Spreadsheet model	A real life situation created on a computer
3.1	What if	Questions that you can ask using a spreadsheet model
3.2	Rules	The basis on which a computer model works
3.3	Autosum	A feature in spreadsheets that automatically adds up numbers
3.3	Sum	Adding up numbers in a spreadsheet
3.3	Test	Making sure something works
3.4	Cell border	The style of the outside edge of a cell
3.4	Cell colour	The background colour of a cell
3.4	Currency	When numbers are shown in pounds and pence, e.g. £10.50
3.4	Format	The way in which information is presented, e.g. the style of the fonts, the use of colours
3.4	Layout	The way that information is positioned on a page
3.4	Text labels	Text used to explain information, e.g. on a graph
3.4	Title	The main heading
3.5	Cost	The amount of money that things are bought for
3.5	Insert	Adding a new row or column into a spreadsheet
3.5	Price	The amount of money that things are sold for

3.5	Profit	The amount of money you make when you sell something
3.6	Prediction	An estimate of something that might happen
3.6	Variable	A piece of information in a spreadsheet that might change
3.7	Bar chart	A style of graph with the data displayed as bars
3.7	Graph	A way of showing numerical information in a visual way
3.7	Graph type	The style used to graph information, e.g. pie chart, bar chart, etc.
3.7	Key	Used to explain any colours used on a graph
3.7	Line graph	A style of graph with the data plotted in a line
3.7	Pie chart	A style of graph with the data displayed in segments of a circle
3.7	Plot	Putting numerical information into a graph
3.7	Scatter plot	A style of graph with the data plotted as dots
4.1	Closed question	A style of question where people are given a choice of answers
4.1	Hypothesis	A prediction of something that might happen
4.1	Open question	A style of question where people can answer how they want
4.1	Questionnaire	A way of collecting information from lots of people
4.2	Data structure	A way of organising information that has been collected
4.2	Data type	The kind of data that is being stored, e.g. text or number
4.2	Date	A type of answer where the format is needed in date form
4.2	Multiple-choice	Where people are given a list of choices when answering a question
4.2	Numeric	Data that is in the form of a number
4.2	Sample size	How many people will fill in a questionnaire
4.2	Sampling	Selecting who you are going to ask to fill in a questionnaire
4.2	Text	A type of answer where the answer is going to be words
4.2	Yes/No	A type of answer where the answer can only be either yes or no
4.3	Database	A collection of data
4.3	Drop-down list	Used to show a list of options in a computer system
4.3	Plausible	Believable
4.3	Range check	A method of checking that a number is within certain limits when it is typed in
4.3	Validation checks	A method of reducing mistakes when data are typed into a database
4.4	AND	Used when searching a database to refine a search
4.4	Ascending	Putting data into order with the lowest item first
4.4	Descending	Putting data into order with the highest item first
4.4	Field	One item of information in a database, e.g. age or gender
4.4	Filter	The process of finding the information you want – used mainly in spreadsheets
4.4	OR	Used when searching a database to expand a search
4.4	Record	Information about one person or object in a database
4.4	Search	The process of finding the information you want
4.4	Sort	The process of putting information into order
4.5	Average	Add several numbers together and divide by the number of items
4.5	Trend	The way that things are going and are expected to go in the future
4.6	Conclusion	Coming to a decision after analysing data
4.6	Report	A way of presenting information – usually used to present a conclusion

5.1	Control	When computers are used to control other things
5.1	Control system	Any system that is controlled by a computer, e.g. a central heating system
5.1	Decision	In control – the computer decides what to do next
5.1	Flowchart	A way of showing how things work, using a diagram
5.1	Input	Data fed into a computer
5.1	No route	In control – the route it follows if something is false
5.1	Output	What comes out of a computer
5.1	Process	The steps the computer goes through
5.1	Program	A list of instructions that a computer follows
5.1	Programmed	A computer that has been given a list of instructions to follow
5.1	Sensor	A device used to measure physical changes
5.1	Yes route	In control – the route it follows if something is true
5.2	Annotation	Writing or typing on something to explain what it is
5.2	Flowchart symbol	One of the shapes used in a flowchart diagram
5.2	Start/Stop	In control – shows the start and end of a flowchart
5.3	Loop	In control – a list of instructions that keep repeating themselves
5.3	Subroutine	In control – a small group of instructions
5.4	Counter	In control – a way of keeping count
5.4	Variable	In control – an item of information that changes, e.g. temperature
5.5	Feedback	Information received in a control system
5.5	Simulation	A real life situation played out on a computer
6.1	Computer-controlled devices	Any piece of equipment that is controlled by a computer
6.2	Attachment	Any file that is sent along with an email
6.2	Blog	A diary kept on the Internet
6.2	Chat room	Several people communicating at the same time over the Internet
6.2	Email	A method of sending and receiving messages electronically
6.2	Messenger service	Several people exchanging messages at the same time over the Internet
6.2	Newsgroup/Forum	An electronic version of a noticeboard
6.2	Social network	A website where people share information about themselves, e.g. MySpace
6.2	Spam	The email version of junk mail
6.2	Video conference	A meeting held on computers using webcams
6.2	Virus	A small program designed to cause damage to a computer
6.3	Cyberbullying	Bullying that takes place over the Internet or using mobile phones
6.3	Personal information	Any information that identifies you personally, e.g. name, address, etc.
6.3	Risk	How likely it is that you are in danger
6.3	Undesirable content	Information and images on websites that are unpleasant or illegal

INDEX